TEENAGER'S

GUIDE

TO

Feminism

A TEENAGER'S GUIDE TO Feminism

Edited by Pear Shaped Press

Pear
Shaped
Press

A Teenager's Guide to Feminism

© 2020 Pear Shaped Press

ISBN13: 978-1-7360522-0-4

Pear Shaped Press
Camas, WA
http://www.pearshapedpress.com

Cover design by Stephanie Anderson
Interior design by Megan Mimiaga

Printed in the United States of America

Hey reader!

As the editors at Pear Shaped Press, we are thrilled to welcome you to *A Teenager's Guide to Feminism*, our very first anthology. Thank you for picking this book up!

From the beginning, our mission as a press has always been centered around a deep commitment to intersectional feminism and storytelling. We seek to bring more stories about women, written mostly by women, to the world. In *A Teenager's Guide to Feminism*, we are specifically seeking to make space for intergenerational conversations about growing up, understanding ourselves, claiming and reclaiming our power, and honoring the women who came before us.

As a press, we are committed to a community-centered approach to publishing. As part of that commitment, we have instituted a community reader program to decentralize editorial control and invite community input. We were lucky enough to assemble an awesome team of community readers to help us make difficult decisions and shape the book into something special that fulfills, and perhaps even surpasses, our collective visions. We are so thankful for the chorus of voices that made this collection possible.

Of course, we can't publish a collection in 2020 without talking about, well, 2020. From the grief and disruptions caused by COVID-19 to the inspiring and necessary reinvigoration of the Black Lives Matter movement, this year has been anything but predictable. At the beginning of the pandemic, we made the difficult decision to postpone the publication of this collection. Though we were disappointed, spending extra time with our contributors and their work to fine tune this book has been a bright light through this difficult time. The events and conversations of 2020 have also reaffirmed our mission — driving commitment to intersectional feminist activism, with specific focus on anti-racist work. As individuals and as an entity, we know we must do more than learn and listen; we must act as collaborators and accomplices in the fight toward true equality.

When we initially dreamed up this collection, we could not have imagined that the final product would feature such incredible work. Our contributors bravely share stories and poems about their own traumas, fears, hopes, and dreams. We were continuously blown away by the incredible variety of work we've had the privilege of featuring in this collection. Wherever you are in your journey, our contributors have something to offer. We hope that you, dear reader, find solace, joy, community, and growth in the pages of this book the way that we have.

All our best,
Pear Shaped Press

Stephanie Anderson,
Christina Brown,
and Megan Mimiaga

TABLE OF CONTENTS

TEEN TALK

WHAT FEMINISM MEANS TO ME

by Sana Asifriyaz

Feminism is:

by definition, the belief that both men and women are equals.
nothing like the way it is stereotypically portrayed.
not women hating men.a global phenomenon for all.
centripetal force for all of mankind, no matter how different we all are.
a fight against injustice.
irresistible.
interesting to discuss.
worth exploring.
positivity.
having a voice and not being too shy to own it.
a source of light in a dark world.
beautifully empowering.
the greatest thing since sliced bread.
much-needed.
life-changing for billions.
something I am grateful for.
misunderstood because of prevalent ignorance.
loathed because it challenges centuries of patriarchal practices.
enlightening.
wonderfully audacious.
meaningful.
nothing to be ashamed of.
a lifestyle.
a voice for the voiceless.
worth being a part of.
my pride.

3

THE WORLD OF MAN

by Hannah Jeoung

for many lifetimes, you have not seen me
for I live inside an opaque box
my delicate china skin is too dear
the bone white of my hands too weak
to ever venture out or near the world of Man

I must have some disease!
something called os-teo-poro-sis?
(I read it from a book, I have so much time)
that breaks my little brittle bones
since I have not been allowed to enter the world of Man

my days are filled with inside things
I sew and read
and take care of those dear things called kids
sometimes you come in and give me fistfuls
of green paper called money
I carefully save these rectangular wafers
although I have colorful papers galore
for they must have come from the world of Man

I have shelves full of beautiful dolls and frilly things
dresses and bonnets and bags
you must also love these beautiful things
as I often hear you say they are why I am lucky
that I do not live in the world of Man

sometimes it gets dark in my little box
and me, myself, and I am all quite alone
I know it is against the rules, but-
I open the window a tiny crack

and gaze into the light of the world of Man
sometimes when I ask to go out
I swear that you almost look scared
maybe that is the reason behind
the bruises and scars on my body
for someone you call precious
you do not always treat me so
perhaps you have learned that from the world of Man

as an apology, I sometimes get stories:
they're full of kings and knights
heroes who save princesses
I know you dream you are like them
and that my salvation is my box
but I see no dragons but you in the world of Man

for now what I can only do is hide inside my little box
but remember that every second I hum and sew,
every minute I cook a meal,
every hour I read a book,
every year I rock a cradle,
I shall be thinking about joining the world of Man

SUFFOCATION

by Yousra Kawsar

This society, this place, this world
suffocates me.
It goes too fast.
It expects too much.
Time slips away like sand
right through your fingers.
Chores, homework AP tests,
problems without solutions
Get A's on all your tests
Why did you miss that shot? The hoop is right there!
Countless sleepless nights
STUDY STUDY STUDY

I am overwhelmed.
"STOP!" I yell *"Please!"*
But time doesn't stop for anyone
and another wave crashes over me.
When can I breathe?

Dear Mr. or Mrs. Police Officer

by Kennedy Reynolds

Do you know who I am?

Do you know how I weep for my brothers and sisters
that have died at your hands?

Do you know how we're killed every single day?

No you don't,
cuz by the way it looks they look no different than me.

We're just a black blur of criminals and thugs whose lives are the equivalent to that of a slug's.

We take to the streets to protest and incite change.

But it seems the route we're going
is the one where we end up in chains.

See, we don't want to hurt you and we don't want your power.

We just wanna be able to bloom like the other white flowers.

As you gun us down and our blood fills the streets, it seeps into the ground as fertilizer under your feet.

Ever since the day when we became free, we ran from your plantations, the air under our feet.

Now as we walk around in what is called a "UNITED" nation, we have to live different from you, not free from your rules and regulations. Now as I finish speaking, giving you a peek into what I'm feeling.

I hope you know how we live as a community
that will not stop kneeling.

CAPRICIOUS BIRD

by Katin Sarner

We are not birds
But we all fly
Drumming up thunder and rain
There is a flash of inspiration
Positively and negatively charged
But the challenge remains the same
I dart from flower to flower
You are often amused by my attempts to take off
But my bold and adaptable ways
Have allowed me to thrive
Starting from scratch
As a tiny tyrant
But crystals need room to grow
Both foreign and intriguing
As layers upon the walls
And endless sunshine
From each door in the birdhouse
How other people have answered this question
We may never fully know
Just lean in and listen
See from above
Remember and honor what is important
Because all that glitters is not gold

OUR BLESSINGS

by Israa Kawsar

All of us feel
we're the victim.
The world is against us,
trying to make our lives
worse than they already are.
We do everything for others,
yet we're still suffering.
Wondering,
when will our good deeds pay off?
When will our luck finally change?
But, are we?
Are we victims of life's unfairness?
Or, do we just tend to focus on everything
that needs to change in our lives?
What about everything we do have?
Is our luck really that bad?
Or, do we just never count our blessings?

A BROKEN BAG OF BONES

by Sophia Moore

they tell us to love ourselves
they swear if you're comfortable in your own skin,
you'll never feel
too skinny
too fat.

well if we love ourselves so much,
tell me why there are girls throwing up their 50 calorie lunch,
tell me why we can never have a conversation
without you bringing up your massive thighs,
tell me why i cried myself to sleep that night,
shaking my bag of bones,
because not only was i told i was "too skinny,"
i finally felt it.

they tell us to love ourselves.
if we do, then why am i not the first one
to be writing these angry words?
why does every girl have to punish herself at the beach
for not fitting into the perfect summer suit?
why is there a personal responsibility for feeling like
you have to bend over backwards to fit an impossibly crafted mold
that has only ever been filled by plastic mannequin
and perfectly photoshopped models?

i see it in every woman i meet,
my mother, my sister, the body connected to my own two feet.
if we are all so happy with ourselves,
with our bodies, with our souls,
then why do we still find
ourselves speaking words like fat and skinny

and chubby and ribby.
they tell us to love ourselves,
and they lie.

they want you to purge your soul to the toilet bowl,
cry yourself to sleep just because
you were larger than the jeans they sold at forever 21.
they want you to run, so far, so fast,
every day just to try to lose some weight.
i guess shin splints are tolerable
when you look like a Victoria Secret model.

they don't care about you,
or your beautifully crafted soul,
they care about the kind of news story your empty body will make,
just so they can pucker up
and do it all again.
they care about the statistic you will make,
how the obesity levels in America are sky high, but
won't you be upset if you skip that drive through McDonald's run?

they care about setting standards for bodies that aren't theirs
bodies that they know are created
proportionally and are perfect as they come, and yet,
these same bodies can have the
measurements of a perfect 36-24-36, just for the fun of it!
they tell us to love ourselves, over and over and over again
why can't they ever mean it?

if we all loved ourselves
our shape and our size and our bodies would be more
than objects and numbers to your
spray-tanned and edited CoverGirl
(does she even know what you've done to her body?
does she even know how far you've distorted her figure
so that it appears she's impossibly thin?
does she know how many girls will look up to her for this,
how many pounds will be shed, how
much damage a couple pounds off the side will cause?
does she care?)

if we all loved ourselves, they wouldn't love themselves.
their parasitic appetite for self-loathing is alarming,

the rate at which they continue to make mannequins thinner and thinner,
and the words that are blasted at us grow harsher:
because Glamour magazine claims that 97% of women
will be cruel to their bodies today!

and what about the boys and men
and their perfectly defined muscles:
"it's just as hard to be Ken as it is to be Barbie"
i hear you, i promise.
of course we love ourselves.

in a world where the "perfect body" is so impossible to attain,
in a world where steroids and waist shapers
are acceptable to gain the results you crave,
in a world where we can't even talk about our bodies anymore
because we've been brainwashed
into thinking that our bodies are not temples,
they are vessels that we can be extreme with
in order to fit the extreme box we're being shoved into.

we love ourselves.
so very much.

"FEMININITY"

by Samyukta Iyer

Femininity knocks on my door late Saturday morning
She wears a neatly ironed dress that reminds me of a picnic blanket
With a giggle and hair toss, she thrusts into my hands
A church pamphlet
A school fundraiser
And a plastic knife

Femininity passes me in the hallway
She wears her quirky t-shirt tucked in, showing off her perfectly flat
and rounded stomach from the abyss of the oversized top
Cuffed jeans and round glasses, her Vans, the bow on top
Close enough to be done, but still too far away

Femininity smiles at me on YouTube
He is wearing eyeliner that stretches to the ends of the earth
Blush that cost a month's rent
And a grin that envelops the cynicism in its warm embrace

Femininity drops off my lunch
With stretch marks, loving thighs
She is a human pillow with the poise of a skyscraper though she barely
scrapes by with 5 feet
She watches Whatsapp videos to fall asleep and writes Rama Nama
when she's worried
She is insecure and self conscious
And it is my job to make sure it doesn't get to her
But femininity stands strong, and with the repetition of a monotonous
alarm tone
She rises for prayer
Femininity crochets on the couch
Watching everything on TV, from bhajans, to soap operas, to cooking

shows with women who probably can't make keerai kutan like her
Covering everyone in her family with the flex of her fingers and the
strength in her eyes
The matriarch of a sprawling banyan tree

Femininity sits in her room
Writes poetry and procrastinates on math homework
Worries too much, wants to be in a musical
Carries the weight of worlds of her broad, manly shoulders
Wears baggy shirts that cover her butt
Wants to tuck in her shirt, tries tucking in her shirt, realizes that the
back will ride up and untucks her shirt
Wants to wear leggings, but one look at her thighs gets rid of that
blasphemy
Feels the balloon of her stomach against the baggiest of shirts
The rubbing of her thighs, like two erasers that desperately want to get
rid of each other
Wears housecoats during the day
Wears pottus and peace signs and prays for power
Over her mind

Femininity is me
Femininity is you
It is expanding
And we are fine

BECOMING MY OWN WOMAN

by Sana Asifriyaz

During my early childhood, I never noticed a difference between men and women. Then, I was indifferent to being a girl. Frankly, I barely even noticed that I was a girl. To me, it was merely a matter of labels. At school, oftentimes, boys and girls would divide themselves into separate groups, like a game of "tug of war." It seemed, to me, like an excuse to categorize people — a means to organize so that identification would be simpler. As in, since there were seven boys and nine girls in the class, there were sixteen students in total. It served to make life easier, didn't it? Everything that I kept mentally rationalizing seemed innocent. If not, I didn't know what it meant to be of either sex.

Several years later, I had begun to see that the separation signifies something far from innocent. It was a distinction between the superior group (men) and the inferior group (women). In our society, being a boy meant that you were physically stronger, emotionally more stable and, therefore, better. On the other hand, being a girl meant that you were the complete opposite and, therefore, not good enough. In fact, teachers, both male and female, would call on boys, whether they were physically strong or weak, to help them lift heavy objects — desks and such — while girls, both physically strong and weak, would remain in their seats silently, maybe even shamefully, feeling futile.

Boys and girls soon began to emphasize how different they looked from each other. Boys were always masculine and girls feminine. Anything else was unacceptable and would be frowned upon. What once seemed to me to be simply a difference in appearance between groups of human beings now became an important part of their respective identities.

As I was in the midst of processing these societally-ingrained views and standards, I realized that others weren't the only ones suffering from these ideals; I too was a victim of these gender roles. I became more

21

conscious that I was a girl, like many others, in a world that favored boys. I began to better understand how deeply this affected us. Around this time, my family had begun to adhere some of their traditional Indian values, namely gender roles, onto me. I was told how a girl should be — shy and modest, gentle, and caring. I remember being told how a boy should be — macho, outspoken, and open. As many of my cousins each started their own families with their spouses, I was even schooled about what often happens after marriage. A woman is to be supportive of her husband, even if it means sacrificing her own career and dreams. She should put her everything into making her marriage successful, keeping her husband happy, and raising capable children. A man, on the other hand, is to be the breadwinner and head of his family. In other words, men and women were to remain in their respective domains. The nostalgic separation of boys and girls now meant something far more severe, and had become a nightmare that I was witnessing and fearing every day.

I was conflicted between my own morals and society's expectations of people, including me. I didn't want to live a life confined to one sphere, or be seen as less than a man. I couldn't wish that upon anyone. I knew I wouldn't comply with these standards and, from there, I grew a passion to voice my opinions against it and for anyone else who would be harmed by these standards.

One of the lessons I learned through this dilemma is that I am a part of a group — women. Clearly, I was no longer the spectator of matters between boys and girls. I was one of the girls all along. The truth is, we are a part of the same group, not just because we are women, but also because many of us share similar experiences and have been told similar things. I gained pride in being one of these individuals because we could share these stories with each other and learn from each others' perspectives. We are one voice in unison, speaking in favor of equality between the sexes.

During this experience, I was able to define what it means to be a woman. Being a woman doesn't necessarily mean being modest and shy, wearing makeup, being weak, and following other such gender roles, or being submissive and repressed. Being a woman isn't insulting. It means being your own individual, finding your own voice, and using it for the good of society. Being a woman means being a global citizen, a human being, and an equal to everyone else. Just because women share an identity doesn't mean that one woman is the same as every other woman in appearance or personality. A woman can look like anyone and be like anyone. There isn't a certain formula to be a woman or even a man. There is a certain formula to being you, and you get to create it for yourself. Each woman is different and unique. But all women have special qualities. A woman is strong-willed, eloquent, and true to herself. A woman has the power to lift herself off the ground when she is put down. A woman is capable of breaking the barriers that limit her. This is what I am capable of and what you are capable of. This is what it means to be a woman.

LETTERS TO THE WOMEN WHO SHAPED US

To You, Women, I am Eternally Grateful

by Karisma Jaini

To the women who shaped me—

It is to you I apologize first. By apologizing to you, I am apologizing to every part of myself that I have been conditioned to hate, a compilation of every feature you have bestowed upon me that I have cast aside and shamed. Through apology, I learn to reconcile with the mistakes I have made.

Mom, grandma, abuela, and every teacher or mentor, every woman before, you have saved me. You have whispered in my ear at my lowest moments, calling me back to you. You have supplied the wisdom to traverse even the darkest of times. You have provided me with the self-love to get out of them, too.

I remember three specific times you came to me,
and saved my life.

One. When my father was diagnosed with stage four.

Two. When my heart was broken for the first time.

Three. When I painted my fingers with my own blood and smiled.

When my father got the terminal label slapped onto his wrist, I didn't know how to react. To be honest, a part of me always knew he would die before I was supposed to graduate from high school. The fancy term "stage four" seemed to seal the deal. Before, I had dismissed the fact that he would die. His death seemed aloof, almost too abstract to even occur. That night, I cried. That same night, I picked myself back up. The knowledge granted to me by you kept me going. I couldn't break apart when the people I loved needed me most. I emulated everything you taught me— power, compassion, and perseverance.

I remember my first heartbreak vividly. I was so young, and really still am. I was so angry with myself. I felt like I poisoned the one that I loved by being around them. I hated myself, and attempted to discard every part of me that was loved by the one that broke my heart. If I erased the source of the poison, then I couldn't hurt anyone else. But you came to me, once more, when my image was so distorted I couldn't see myself in a mirror. I remember that night, only a lamp was on, and the garish façade was consuming the parts of you that I cherished. Every part of myself that I loved, every part of myself that you gave me, was being erased. I wanted to peel back that ugly skin and scream, but instead, I ate something that you would make me, something full of warmth and full of fat and joy, and decided to put that fake skin to rest.

I have felt so repulsed by my own appearance that I have tried to cut it out myself. Tried to scratch myself out of my skin because it just wasn't good enough compared to the people around me. The people around me were beautiful, inside and out. Their minds were satiated and tranquil, their bodies the image of Western glamour. I could never be something as alluring, or brilliant. For a crime that grave, I had to be punished. I cut the ugly out of my skin and smiled as I watched it drip out, red and gorgeous like the girls I wanted to embody. Distantly, I could feel you crying. I was snapped back into reality by the remnants of your will and the ghost of your ferocity. From that moment I pledged to love myself, and the scars that came along with me.

Mom, grandma, abuela, every teacher and mentor, every woman that came before me, shaped me—I now stand before you in pride. I am proud to call myself a strong young woman. I am grateful to face the world as you would: with wit and will, with grace and compassion. I am proud to walk the body you gave me and am proud to see the characteristics I admired in you manifesting within myself. My past is concrete. My present is littered with uncertainty, and the fleeting joy of the moment. But because of you, my future is limitless.

To you, women, I am eternally grateful.

With love,
Karisma

To My Mother and My Aunt

by Julia Cheng

To my mother and my aunt,

To the two women who showed me how to fight for what you believe in and work hard for what you want out of life. These incredible women demonstrated how to be strong in their own ways, and from them I have learned my own strength.

My mother, a true romantic, fought for what she was passionate about, whether it was her art as a playwright or her relationships. She has never been afraid to be deeply vulnerable and honest about her emotions. My mother taught me to strive for kindness and empathy in everything I do.

My aunt is a wonderful dichotomy of pragmatism and creativity. She expertly crafts life plans around how she envisions her end goals and somehow makes time to stop and paint the roses. My aunt inspires me to be brazenly ambitious and appreciate beautiful moments within the chaos of life.

I'm so thankful to these women for how much they have taught me. They are both public school teachers, and their instinct to help others and model good behavior for others inspires me to be a better person in this world. They taught me to work hard for what I believe in, like my passion for writing.

Through their successes, as well as their failures, they have offered me guidance on how I can live without regrets. My aunt took me on college tours and pushed me to try business and art classes to make sure I explored all of my options. My mother gave almost no restrictions for me besides attending college, telling me she'd be proud of me no matter what I choose to do in life after graduation.

With love,
Julia

THE GRACE OF GIRLFRIENDS

by Ra Avis

My girlfriends are sharp-angled rusted tin.
Sharks in the reef. Spike and scale,
lumbering tails that swat and clear.

My girlfriends are bumble bee soft, killer bee buzzing.
Salt. Sugar. Ground cayenne in the ear.
Cinnamon in hot milk tea.

My girlfriends are the open sea,
siren-screeching,
star-filled,
made of current and turn,
drowning the men,
lifting the tide.

They break their feet in water, smash bone to wing,
to fly, to drive.
My girlfriends are unashamedly driven.

My girlfriends are scotch that punches the throat,
kisses fluttered over a skinned knee,
a skinned knee, a punch, a throat. A shape.

A sharp I shaped myself on.

The bells that call me home.

My girlfriends are architect and palm and they build me tall,
smash me through ceilings,
monument me through frozen and fires
and four-lane freeways.

My girlfriends are traditionalists.
They pull fresh cookies from the oven and say
I like your dress,
and I give thanks.

We wash the blood and grit from our body,
set aside our skin and spears, set the table,
set our intentions.

We say grace for each other.
We are grace for each other.
And I give thanks.

The cookies are perfect.
We dissolve them into us.

Perfection into perfection.
Amen.

A Letter to the Woman Who Inspires Me Most

by Jazzminn Morecraft

The individual that has inspired me most is my mama. Besides the fact that she is an outstanding individual, she is a mom, a wife, and a boss. She has raised three kids, all while going to school (twice!), and has progressed in her successful career.

I know a lot of individuals can say the same thing about at least one of their parents as well, but I think fewer could also say that the parent that has inspired them is also their stepparent. It seems nowadays that stepparents have this stigma around them, as if the "step" in front of their name makes them any less of a parent. However, this could not be further from the truth in my situation.

Mama,

I am speaking directly to you now. Let me tell you a story that may sound familiar.

A young woman (around twenty) makes a bet with a man that she works with at a restaurant. This bet is that she can't make a certain amount of tips in a shift on one night. He says, if she does, he will wash her car for her. When the night comes to an end, and the tips are counted, victory is in hand for her, and the man then has to wash her car.

I know this story is familiar to you, as it is the story of you and daddy. Shortly after this, as you guys have told us (the kids), you started to date. I always loved to hear this story, because it is a point in time when one thing altered the lives of many. It also has been a story that has inspired me because you chose to stay with this man, a man thirteen years older than you, as well as a man that already had two kids. You did not shy away, but rather embraced it and treated us (my brother and me) as your own.

Now, I don't remember much from then, as I was three, but I can only imagine that it couldn't have been the easiest. You were younger than I am today, and to put myself in your shoes definitely scares me a little bit. However, you did not only survive, you thrived!

While thriving, you also had a kid. But this changed nothing. This did not cause the love you had for my brother and I to disappear or shrink, but rather it seems your heart grew to accommodate all three of your children. You have treated all three of us the exact same, showered all three of us with the same love, and I can say I have never felt like I was any less your child than the one that you physically had.

You have been in my life for the majority of it, around twenty years so far (does that make you feel old?), but I always say you have been in my life for all of it! You are constantly there to help and support me through the tough times. You are forever my unwavering rock. You tell me the truth, even when it's brutal. You listen to me rant when I am having a bad day, and brag when it is a good one. You share in my triumphs and help me through the bumps, and are always encouraging me to keep my head up.

When we meet new people you never introduce me as your STEP-daughter, but rather as your daughter, and I cannot put into words the feeling that I have because of that. Everyone just sees us as mother and daughter (that do lots together). So, while technically, you are my step-mom, I would just like to stress that, you are so much more than that!

You are an individual who has shown me resilience and that, with hard work and perseverance, I can achieve anything that I set my mind to. You have shown me that it is okay for your emotions to show and that taking time to clear your head is not a bad thing. You have shown me that it is okay to make mistakes and that you can learn from those mistakes. You have been real and honest with me about the good times and the bad times. You are the best example of what a strong woman is!

Overall, I just want to thank you. I know that soon I will have to start my next chapter, one that will take place a little further from you than I am used to. So, before that time comes, I want to make sure you know how important you are to me, and how important you will continue to be. I want you to know that you have impacted me, and that you can trust me to make the right decisions because you taught me the way to do so.

Thank you for always answering my text messages and picking up the phone when I call, no matter how lame the reason I called or even if I could have told you what I needed to in a text. Thank you for being the best example I could have, and providing me with the tools I will need to not only be successful but to be a decent human being as well (even if you did not know that you were giving them to me). Thank you for being my shoulder to cry on and the bestest friend that I have ever had, and for listening to me tell the same story a million times. Thank you for all the faith that you have in me. And thank you for taking a bet with a man, even knowing that he was placing a losing bet!

Thank you for being you! I love you the most!

Love,
Jazzminn

P.S. Even though I feel like I have to some small degree shared with you the impact you have had on me and how absolutely thankful I am for you, I am still left feeling like it is not enough, and I don't believe it ever will be. You deserve the world mama, but since I cannot give that to you, no matter how much I wish I could, I give you this letter that hopefully shows and reminds you that you have been, and always will be, such an important part of my life.

To the woman who didn't have to love me but chooses to every day, THANK YOU!

TO THE TEACHERS

by Katin Sarner

To the teachers who have helped me grow into the passionate young woman I am today,

I want you all to know that you are my heroes. Teachers are who we owe our knowledge to. Not only knowledge of math or history, but knowledge of the ever changing world before us. They prepare us for a world outside of textbooks and homework with encouragement, support, and inspiration. I have had a magnitude of teachers thus far in my education, but you three women are the teachers who have made an unbelievably inspirational impact on my life, and whom I respect with such admiration.

Mrs. Leisy,

When I entered your class in the fifth grade, I was convinced that I was stupid because I couldn't do long divison. Every problem you gave our class felt like a brick weighing me down. I tried my hardest, but the numbers never made sense.

I remember one day while I was doing my math work at my desk, I got very frustrated with myself. At that moment, I thought my "long lived" math career was over. I resented addition and subtraction, but I could manage. My times tables were rough, but I still passed the fourth grade. Except, this time I was certain that long division would be the death of me. I looked up at you, and said I couldn't do it. You looked into my eyes and calmly said, "try again."

Not once did you let me give up. Time after time again, I failed, but you spent time with me explaining every step, until I eventually understood the concept. I started the fifth grade thinking that I was a complete idiot, and that I would never be as smart as the other kids in class. I ended the fifth grade knowing that I am capable of anything I set my mind to.

Six years later, I am in my Junior year of highschool and have never gotten less than an "A" in math. I still absolutely hate it, but every time I fail, I try again, and eventually get the right answer. A day does not go by in Algebra II without me remembering your support and encouragement during the fifth grade. I cherish the minimal memories I still retain from math in Room 14, as they serve as motivation in all aspects of my life.

Thank you, Mrs. Liesy, for helping me realize that a thought is not indefinite, and a difficult problem is not impossible.

Mrs. Liebfried,

I walked into my first day of seventh grade, intimidated by the woman standing by the door wearing bright pink glasses. She was standing strong, with confidence practically glowing from her skin. I took a seat in the corner of Room 411 and waited for the bell to ring, announcing the start of class. The woman with the pink glasses walked to the front of the classroom and began explaining what the year would look like in seventh grade Language Arts. That woman was you, Mrs. Leibfried.

I began to admire you, not only as a teacher, but as a person. You never seemed to worry about what others thought of you. You expressed your feelings and opinions powerfully, yet with such grace and dignity. I enjoyed your class tremendously, and began to find joy in writing the essays you assigned, as opposed to viewing them merely as a grade. It was then that I began to understand that I was not just a student, I was a writer, and writing would soon become my savior.

The next year, you were my journalism teacher. You appointed me Editor-in-Chief of our school's newspaper. I woke up everyday with pure excitement, knowing that I had your first period journalism class. You never hesitated to tell me, "Katin, you are going to do so much with your life. You are capable of absolutely anything." I began to believe you and realized that my life was a fresh canvas ready to be painted.

The rest of eighth grade came and left, but during my first few weeks of freshman year, I was diagnosed with Anorexia Nervosa and rushed to the hospital. I felt broken. What started as "just cutting out sugar," turned into an uncontrollable beast, convincing my mind that starvation was power. As the numbers on the scale decreased, it seemed as though the value of my life reduced as well. In my mind, my world was nothing but a mere battle from dressing room mirrors to my newfound infatuation with appetite suppressants.

As I was lying in my hospital bed, a mere shadow of the lively little girl you knew me as, you stepped into my room. For the first time in weeks, my mouth formed a smile. You stayed with me for hours that afternoon, keeping my mind off of the blood pressure cuffs and hospital gowns. We reminisced over memories from your class, bringing a bit of sunshine into my dreary hospital room. You kept telling me, "Katin, you don't have to do this to yourself. You have so much in store for your future." You emphasized how much I would be losing by succumbing to my eating disorder, and most importantly, reminded me of how much I am loved by those around me.

To this day, you never fail to keep in touch. I cherish our conversations, whether that be through text, over brunch, or when I visit your classroom. You have made such an amazing impact on my life, as you have shown me how I can shape my future into anything my heart desires. I am so grateful that you are, and always will be, a part of my life.

Ms. Balliet,

Sophomore year was filled with an abundance of emotions, not only relapsing and reentering intensive outpatient eating disorder treatment, but also facing a traumatic experience that you helped me through with such passion and nurture. Additionally, you taught the class that inspired me in all aspects of my life: English II Honors.

As the year progressed, I began to feel increasingly connected to the material you exposed our class to while reading both *Jane Eyre* and *The Handmaid's Tale*. "Feminism" had never been a word I put much thought into. I knew that I believed in equal rights and felt ardent towards women's representation in government, but I had never felt pertinent regarding the word itself. Except, the more we studied the topic, the more I became aware of the everyday ramifications of being a teenage girl in our current society. I started to feel exceedingly passionate towards equal treatment among the sexes.

One day, while we were studying *The Handmaid's Tale*, I suddenly felt as though the novel, and our discussions surrounding the overall theme, pertained to recent feelings and experiences that seemed to dominate my life. In the few months I had been attending my new highschool, I had somehow managed to end up with a boyfriend. The relationship, however, had me trapped in the forceful grip of a boy who seemed to believe that women are nothing but malleable, weak sexual objects designed to subsist purely for a man's own satisfaction and

39

power. I thought that I was overreacting for feeling unsafe, or that what was happening to me was my own fault. However, our class content proved otherwise: I began to understand that I was a victim of sexual assault, and that I was still trapped in an abusive relationship.

I remember sending you an email, frantically, at 2:00am one Sunday morning just days before school let out for summer, asking if I could talk to you the next day. My boyfriend broke up with me; I was relieved. My wall of self-protection crumbled into a pile of fear, terror, and shame. After our emotionally involved year in English II Honors, I knew that you would believe me. While studying articles in class regarding sexual assault, I could see how much empathy you felt towards the individuals experiencing such trauma, as well as the raving indignation you possessed towards their assailants. You were the person to go to about the confusion and utter fear my mind contained.

That day, I felt emotions I never knew existed in such an intense way. I was left helpless, without a clear path to follow, so I got into my car and drove, without any destination in mind, crying and screaming at the top of my lungs in frustration. I could not stand existing in the body he violated. After driving for what seemed like an eternity, I eventually found a parking spot, took a deep breath, and dialed your number with mascara running down my face. When you answered the phone, I didn't know what to say or where to start; it seemed as though I couldn't remember how to speak. You helped me calm down and promised that you would not judge me for anything I told you. Suddenly, the words came bursting out of me, like a soda can finally exploding after having been tossed around for much too long. All of the fear and pain I had been denying for so long rose to the surface as I began to explain the traumatic events I experienced over the past few months.

You validated my emotions. You told me I was not alone. You made sure that I felt safe and protected. You said time after time, with such empathy, "You did nothing wrong. He did." Not many teachers would take hours out of their Sunday afternoon to support a student like that.

Since that day, you have never stopped fighting for me, regardless of what others tell you. When several people around me did not hold my truth to the extent of recognition it deserved, you fervidly advocated for me and my sense of security, practically risking your job. You communicated with me authentically and treated me like an adult, rather than a broken little girl. You offered me a safe place at school when being on the same campus as him was too much, taking the time each day to listen as I processed the fear. You were, and still are, there for me, day or night, no matter what. I cannot thank you enough for that.

In addition to your benevolence, you have given me a whole new perspective on the society in which we reside. I now realize that there needs to be more people like you in this world: individuals who unconditionally fight for justice. You help so many people at our school, myself included, find their voice. Once again, I cannot even begin to express how grateful I am for you. I will never forget your passion.

Katin

Letter to the Woman Who Shaped Me

by Alisha Saxena

Ma,

It's shocking, but we've only got a month together before I embark on the largest adventure of my life. Yes, college comes with new experiences and opportunities, but the deal would have been sweeter if I could have done it with you by my side. But as you say, it's a part of growing up. As I spend my last few weeks in the comfort of my home, I have focused on spending time with everyone, learning new things, and reflecting on my past and present. The time I allocated to reflection has underscored the great impact you, Dad, and Didi have had on my perception of life. Our connection, specifically you and I, has been special in the last few years—I remember the day I took that first step in confiding in you and making you my best friend. I thank myself every day for that foundational moment which started the best friendship I will ever have. You are my genuine best friend forever.

I will not undervalue myself. You constantly remind me that I am not less than the people who I once idolized. My intellect, social abilities, and drive is no weaker than theirs—it might just come in a different shape and form. You taught me that there is more than one path to success, and that there is no need to fret if I have not taken the same steps as someone else. Even more important, once I do reach success, there should not be an impulse to undervalue my achievements just because I forged a different, possibly unconventional path. My journey is mine and mine only—nobody else should be given the power to dictate it.

Relationships are complicated. You and I have talked a lot about the dynamics of friendships and partnerships, and how it will not be perfect.

I should not be afraid to seek new bonds, and should not let the experiences of my past be cinder blocks to future endeavors. Rather, they should be learning opportunities to strengthen the foundation which I build my relationships on. You will never let me forget that I need to also value my time, by not letting my schedule always be the one moved around to fit in social engagements. And yes, I won't let myself get consumed in speculation of "what if," and will put my mind to ease by focusing my attention on something that actually matters in the long run.

I will choose my battles. I have had many phases, from benevolent to the stubborn girl who argues every little point. Though I have not mastered this lesson yet, I am on my way to understanding how to pick my battles—I have to think big picture, and if it will even matter a few days from now. So, arguing over something trivial is achieving nothing but spiking my blood pressure. You have managed to be thick-skinned to such arguments, and I hope to develop a similar resilience.

Now is the time to have fun. The workaholic in me wants to speedily get through these youthful years in order to start a successful career in what I am passionate about, but you have always preached a life of balance. You preach that living your life out with someone is much more joyful than being alone—there is a life beyond work. Also, yes, I will do my best to not be so close-minded about particular experiences in college, and will create some memories for the books.

Yoga. We rediscovered it together, and have undergone this physical and mental revamping for the past few months. I have found much more joy in doing this with you, and you are the reason I was able to further my learning and get certified in yin. Here's where I request that you keep it as a top priority even during your hectic work season, and when I am not there to do it with you.

There are so many more inspirational thoughts you have cemented in my head, in regards to life, politics, yoga, and who knows what else—I learn something new from you every day. I chose these few precepts because these have changed my life the most, turning me from a discontent, apathetic teenager to an optimistic, engaged adult who will not shy away from a challenge. I know that, in the heat of the moment, I may sometimes be too blinded to remember these key lessons, but that's why I have you. Although I will not be able to rest my head on you, hug, and kiss you goodnight every day, technology will hopefully make me feel like I am within arm's reach of you. So, when I call you about something irritating me, or when I call you about feeling homesick, I go in with confidence because I know that you will say just the right thing to get me to snap out of it and continue on with my youthful life.

You have done so much for me, beyond society's tasks for mothers. The emotional enlightenment you have given me is priceless, and words aren't enough to describe the light that will continue to shine on my journey as a result. You are always going to be the most influential woman and person in my life—you are my everything, Ma.

Love you lots,
Alisha

TOUGH STUFF

GINGERBREAD HOUSES

by Aruni Wijesinghe

They came like mice to nibble
what took me a lifetime to build.
The world is cruel to an
unattractive woman who likes
baked goods.

Banished to the fringes of the
village, I tried to construct a
new life of icing sugar and
cookie dough, tried to find some
sweetness again.

What were their names - Handful
and Gristle? The conniving imps
snapped off pieces of the roof and
ate the windows. They crammed
their greedy mouths with my
home, filled their bellies on my
dreams.

Easy to find fault with a
woman who tries to feed
her own hungers. They
called me witch,
cannibal, monster. But
those kids took the first
bites.

*First published in the LA Expressions reading series zine "A Moment of Your Time," March 2019

Self-Portrait in One Broad Meandering Stroke

by Marc Cid

"I'm not like all those other guys,"
says the guy like all those other guys,
but I say:

deep down no I know I'm no different
than he him they them *hes*
who say *women*
with a sigh beforehand
say *woman*
as an accusation or with a my
say *women* with an *our*
say *our womenfolk* like livestock
like stocks rise and fall as they're traded
exchanged change value devalue like the stocks
wooden splintery in the town square to shame blame and burn
these *bitches* these *witches* these *women*
take a sip a swig a shot
of scotch whiskey sigh and tap the bar say *women*
like a full sentence pointed with a period pyre wrapped
in barbed wire implications a trench system code we men

real men dive hide scurry from boob butt baby
bella donna bombardment

feet rotting in river nile crocodile tear dropped flood of muck because
of *women*

says them they him he says some part of me when I see her with him
and wonder

51

will she be safe as if she is x where x is equal to ex is equal to XX
chromosomes

I say *women* with a sigh
I've seen them sigh *women*
I've seen them shame *women*
I've seen them burn *women*
I know deep down
no

Unbeautiful

by Aruni Wijesinghe

no cornflower-blue eyes instead
burning embers more suited to
kohl than mascara brows arched
in perpetual surprise

no golden hair that feathers perfectly
à la Farrah Fawcett repeatedly tucks
the same loose strand behind her right
ear

Maybelline ads are wasted here.

She's not beautiful. self-conscious about the
gap in her front teeth maybe she smiles
anyway

no endless supply of Fair and
Lovely Lightening Cream will
fade cinnamon skin, bark of some
other rare tree

dip of waist flaring to
fecund curves prized
in the tropics, not
here in this City of
Angels

No two-inch thigh gap here.

speaks quietly, sotto voce lean in to catch
every word pronounced lisp at once child-like

and sexy sudden laugh loud as a stack of
plates breaking

She is no classic beauty,
yet haunting in her every
imperfection.

The world drab without her,
this unbeautiful girl.

*First published in The Altadena Poetry Review 2019 (Shabda Press); upcoming in Ac-
colades: A Women Who Submit Anthology (Jamii Publishing, 2020).

Tillandsia

by Amon Elise

My Venus
told me once
that she'll never be a flower.
And I as her daughter,
am expected of more.
Denied the choice of division,
I am wrapped within her.
She spreads her vines
to confine whom she chooses to keep.
Those flies don't even know they're devoured.
Forced to feed the undefeated.
I am supposed to grow in her shadow,
and bloom before her.
As she grows older
is it I who will loan her my nutrients
with these wisps of roots?
Evolved in air,
if I just wait for that final winter,
maybe my daughters,
will have a chance
to learn the danger of soil.

COULDA FOR GOT

by Amon Elise

He ain't have no face.

Coulda been Herald,
coulda been Keith,
coulda been Evan,
but it was Derrick.

Knew it by the hand print
on my thigh's back.
Split themselves open

for questions,
for photographs,
for samples.

These men in blue
charged up to put em in orange,
made sure we all had it coming.

Got caught,
got fingered,
got processed.

CYCLE

by Abigail Ramsey

The heat of the concrete absorbing the summer sun hit my forehead, arms, hips, and legs as my body slammed against it. My forehead stung, and my ankle throbbed. In that short moment between standing and laying on scorching pavement, I had forgotten where I was. When my vision returned and my eyes readjusted to the bright sun, all I could see was him standing over me. His six and a half foot frame towered over my body lying on the ground. His light skin was red from the heat of the sun, and his blonde hair was out of its slicked-back place.

I looked around me to help me remember where we were. The water in the community pool hit the edge with a splash that should have been comforting. There were a few bright pink leaves floating towards the filter. The white bars of the fence surrounding the pool matched the white chairs, white tables, and white pool tiles. The sun reflecting against it was too radiant, but I couldn't tell if I was wincing from the pain or from the overwhelming brightness.

He stood over me with his hand outstretched. His eyes were empty though; I could never recognize him in these moments. The moments after, when there was just a slight realization that things were not what they should be. Those were fleeting moments though. I grabbed his hand, and pulled myself up, my eyes sealed shut to help me ignore the reality of my body. I put weight on my ankle as I started to walk up the step I had fallen down, but the pain, shooting up from the heel of my foot to my knee, sent me to the concrete again.

A family was walking to the white gate of the community pool. I felt their eyes on me, all six of them. The mom seemed more concerned that there was a young couple at the pool alone. Two young girls with her stared at me, but carried on their conversation with each other; their bellowing laughter felt like it was directed at me.

"Everything all right?" the mom yelled over to us.

"Oh yeah, just a bit of a slip!" he yelled back to her. His eyes became welcoming as they turned into a smile. I looked up from my hands massaging my ankles to direct my own fake smile towards them.

He pulled me up, and let me rest my weight on him. I followed him over to the table that we had set our water, sunscreen, house keys, and unused towels on. He gathered his things in his arms, and I limped around the table and did the same. He gave me his hand and led me out of the gated community pool. Home was just a few doors down, after you passed the other four houses with white stucco and perfect yards, maintained by people who only worked in these types of neighborhoods. Each house, with its two stories, large windows, and freshly painted shutters, felt like it was staring at me.

"We can get you some ice back at the house," he said. I nodded in response without looking up at him. My eyes were fixated on my bare feet limping their way down the light grey sidewalk bordered with bright green, perfectly trimmed grass. After fiddling with his keys while I leaned against his shoulder, he unlocked the front door. The tile in the entryway felt shockingly cold after walking on the hot cement. As he placed the towels and sunscreen near the front door, I thought about the steps I would have to walk down to get to their kitchen and winced. The steps no more than a foot tall, seemed impassable. Before I started walking, he scooped me up in his arms, my arms wrapped around his neck. I couldn't help but laugh as he carried me from the front door to the living room connected to the kitchen. He gently placed me on the soft brown fabric of the sofa and lifted the recliner. The blanket draped over the arm of the sofa was quickly draped over me.

The sound of ice clinking against itself echoed behind me. His bare feet scratched against the hardwood floor as he moved back to the sofa. He collapsed into the space next to me and handed me the bag of ice. His green eyes met mine; they weren't empty anymore. Without a word, I rested my head on his shoulder and wrapped the bag of ice around my ankle.

"I'm sorry. You, just, should have told me before," he said.

"Yeah, I'm sorry," I said, as I thought about my plans for tomorrow that had made him so angry. I didn't tell him I would be with my sister. She was taking me to Disneyland to celebrate the end of school. We were over a month late for that celebration, but it was hard to balance him and her. My ankle seemed to swell at just the thought of walking around Disneyland all day.

Early the next morning, I wrapped my ankle in an ace bandage. It made it difficult to fit into my shoes normally, but I was determined to fake it. My sister pulled into his driveway that matched the hundreds of other driveways around us, and I limped towards the passenger side door.

After the long drive to the park, my ankle was throbbing more than ever, but I ignored it. Asking her to slow down or go to first aid for me to ice it would be too much of a burden. It would open the door to questions too, which I didn't know how to answer. I limped my way through most of the day. After lunch we rode the carousel, but as I shifted my weight to get off the wooden carousel horse, I shifted the wrong way. The pain shot up to my knee; I closed my eyes and could only see the overwhelming whiteness of the community pool. When I opened my eyes, I was on the floor of the carousel, wooden horse hooves hanging over me. My sister yelled, and a staff member rushed over.

"Hello, ma'am, we are going to get you over to First Aid okay?" the staff member said in a much too cheery tone.

The first aid room was set up with blue padded patient beds against two walls. The walls were painted blue, and my sister sat in the bed against the wall opposite to me. Her face annoyed me. Her eyes were too kind, and her eyebrows tilted in a way to show me pity.

"You know it's going to keep happening right?" she asked, her eyes still staring right at me.

Before I could answer, the staff entered behind a wheelchair that had "Property of Disneyland Resort" scrawled across the back. My sister helped me into it, and we were off on the rest of our day full of laughter. When I came home that night, he cuddled up against me, whispering kind words. He promised it would never happen again.

Two weeks later, the pain of a broken rib pressed against my lungs. I thought I would suffocate right there at the bottom of the carpeted staircase, with my nose and cheeks pressed against the white tile of the perfect entryway in the perfect home.

LIFE STORY

by Charlotte Shao

If the plot of your life does not outline itself for you,
do not despair. Take your pen and write one yourself.
Keep moving, keep going, one beat at a time.
Brace the slow parts, the sad parts, it will add up.
You'll find they weave together the scene you want.
If you look back, wanting nothing more than
to tear out the pages and burn the chapters of
who you once were, don't. Every sentence is important to
who you are now, who you're going to be.
Know that if your book is not closed, your arc is not over.
There is still time to fall in love with your own character.
And as they read, someone else will too.

Raising a Boy

by Eve Lyons

When we have tickle fights
it's a lesson in when you say stop, I stop
even as he keeps coming back for more.

In men's rooms I watch him enter the stall
then guard the door like a lioness.
One in six boys, one in six.

At six, my son already mansplains
takes up too much space when sharing a bed.

As a black man I want his voice to matter.
As a man he needs to shut the fuck up.

My son likes to wrestle all his friends:
With Aidan no one ever seems unhappy
or goes too far. Soulmates.
With Ana it's almost as perfect.
But Noah gets angry if he thinks he's losing,
Joe is fine until he's not, you can see it in his face.
Ella doesn't wrestle at all,
but they will dance together every night.

It's so important to know
who likes what, and when.
Sometimes people change their minds.

I wonder who will stick around for the hard years
wonder whether he'll date them some day.
"White girls get you fifty."
He can't help who he's attracted to.
He must establish consent
every single time.

DEAR TEENAGE ME

Dear Molly

by Molly Scott

Dear Molly (at so many different ages),

I wish so badly I could find you on the blacktop at OLL in first grade and give you a hug. I want to cup our little face and tell you that the haircut from first grade won't last forever (but you'll get it again when you're 27 and love it), that we do like that best friend and it's okay that she's a girl, that your body carries weight and not worth, and that no one else's love will replace what you missed from your fathers.

I want to tell you that neither your biological father nor the one who raised you will ever tell you the things you want to hear (not by the time we're 27, anyways), and that does not mean that you are worthless. They were hurt boys who turned into hurt men who hurt other people along the way, and you have two amazing women in your life who love you with no bounds.

I want to warn you that we will feel very deeply in our lives and we will feel deeply young. I want to tell you that no matter how much you are hurting, you cannot take those scissors into the bathroom stall and cut yourself. You are worth more than that and you don't deserve that. I want to tell you to tell Mom before a friend tells the teacher in seventh grade, who in turn tells Mom, who just can't handle it.

Or better yet, when Mom makes you go to therapy, talk. Open up. Tell them how you feel, because you deserve to try to feel better so much earlier than we eventually do. I also want to tell you that although it might hurt (a lot) at times, you are blessed to feel so deeply because you feel moments that other people don't get to. You get to feel music swim through your hair and bring you nostalgia so strong you can smell the air of Stafford Lake the summer of seventh grade, or feel the sweat dripping down your neck after PE with your head on your desk and the fan running overhead.

I want to tell you that you need to tell yourself "I love you," when you look in the mirror every. single. day. That your body will look different than most girls at school and most of your friends, and that's okay. You don't need to try to have an eating disorder, you shouldn't treat your body like that, because it's only ever good to you. You won't feel better by depriving yourself of food, and you won't feel prettier after trying to make yourself throw up. You will spend a lot of time wishing you had a different body, but every year you will look back and say, "Wow. I looked good, I wish I knew that then and enjoyed it." Our tummy is soft, our skin is supple, our thighs still carry the strength they developed in elementary gymnastics, our arms hold the people we love, our hands create beautiful art and write stirring words, our feet have walked us so many places and into so many memories (and out of places and lives that no longer served us); our body is love.

I want to tell you that you need to spend all the time you will waste on boys, fairweather friends, and trying to be what you think they want you to be, on yourself (...and maybe other girls, it would have been nice to realize that earlier). Keep drawing, keep playing, keep finding the things you love; it is not them. I want to tell you that you will let too many boys in, you'll let too many boys touch you and take you down. You don't need to do that, you don't need to let boys treat you unkindly or use your body to get a taste of acceptance or love. Lips on lips and fingers on skin doesn't mean love, a lot of the time you will just be a body. Don't be a body to anyone, don't let anyone take your power or waste your time or dampen your value. *They don't deserve you.*

Stop trying to repair broken people because they don't want to be fixed. Instead, repair the wounds you never let heal. Put bandaids on the cuts and bruises you kept pinching, picking, and tearing at because you will be here with yourself at the end of the day; they won't be.

Fill the cracks with fruit and paint and watching for shooting stars and Sailor Moon comic books. You gave up on the sketch pads and voice lessons and replaced them with people who wouldn't listen or even last ten years. Lay your seeds where they will be watered, fed, tended to, and nurtured. Stop looking for an oasis in the desert, it's right here inside of you.

Love Forever,
You, but 27

70

Blackness, Feminism, and Life in Between: A Letter to My Teenage Self

by Queen Ex

Dear young Queenie,

I wish to hold you warm and close with these words of truth and wisdom. With these words, I pray you learn LIFE and survival because, although this world is not made to keep you, you are a keeper of this world, and you must create a safe space for those who can survive it. Now, Queenie, listen up, as I explain to you how to navigate life in between your Blackness and your femininity.

Primarily, there is always a question of identity present and you must remain aware of that. When asked who we are, we tend to inadequately answer with a what: an emotion, an occupation, a title, a name. As intelligent beings, we have yet to describe a qualifying set of words that answer this question. Indeed, Queenie, you are more than what any word can be a metaphor for. Indescribable. Priceless. All that and a bag of chips, plus a dab of hot sauce. You are these and more. Still, on this earthly plane, you will identify as two things: Black and Woman. Though you may feel like they are two different things, they are still categories under which you fit and must learn to accept, love, and nurture.

Queenie, you'll find power in being a woman, but not before you find power in being Black. Some may argue the point that perhaps you should be a woman first and support womankind, and that is okay too. Embracing your femininity as a natural-born woman means reaching goddess status, and there is no being more beautiful, strong, and capable. Falling in love with your mind, body, and soul is key to understanding what makes you a force. Commanding your wiles and carrying yourself as a virtuous woman is an intoxicating experience and you, my love, have exactly what it takes to love yourself into your greatest form. Embracing what it means to be Woman is developing the tools to uplift, mobilize, inspire, and lead an entire nation of men, women, and children, even if that nation is your own lineage. Still, Queenie, there is no denying the Blackness in your DNA, and that means something entirely different than what it means to be Woman.

Being Woman means nurturing yourself and educating your family. Being Woman means knowing men like you know women (but don't let the guys know!). Being Woman means exercising wisdom and discernment. It means understanding your power and then knowing when and how to use it. Being Woman means embodying every emotion on the planet and walking in the envy of man. Being Woman means being the living, breathing archetype of everything from countries to cars. Being Woman means holding the sun in your smile and the stars in your eyes. Being Woman means caring for the mounds, canyons, rivers, and plains that landscape your body. Being Woman is standing in virtue, respect, and nobility. Being Woman is knowing Love, but it is also knowing what it means to be hated. Being Woman is being objectified and subject to misuse and under-utilization. Being Woman means being doubted. Being Woman means not being good enough...ever. Being Woman means your strength, wit, and intelligence are contested at every turn. Being Woman means second-class citizenship and being discounted. It is having your kindness and compassion mistaken as weakness. It is having a menstrual cycle that could cripple Hercules every single month. Being Woman is then having hot flashes during menopause that would give Schwarzenegger a tan. Being Woman is birthing every human being on this planet and still having your vagina synonymous with fragility. These things are what it means to really, truly be Woman.

Now, to walk a life of a Black person is to love yourself just enough to have it not inconvenience anyone else. Being Black means wanting to educate your family without having received the education yourself. Being Black means division of various kinds is normal. Being Black means having to awaken into your power after not knowing it was there all along. Being Black means to hide your truest emotions or find a way to express them intelligently so as to not sound off the Nigga Alarm other races are so eager to set off. Being Black means watching mainstream media enjoy your culture and defame you at the same time. Being Black is knowing your ancestors contributed so much to this country and dealing with your deep disdain for its lack of appreciation for it. Being Black means knowing you are still worth a third of a person when no one wants to make room for you on the sidewalk. Being Black is wondering if you'll die every time you get pulled over. Being Black is having "the talk" with your children and teaching them how to behave with little faith that it will matter in the grand scheme of things. Being Black is being a stand-up citizen and still feeling the risk of driving/walking/swimming/playing/gathering while Black. Being Black means having the sun in your hair and the universe in your soul and still wondering if you are great enough or worthy enough to have your actual life mean something to someone else. Being Black is standing in solidarity for your people while being forced to choose between consent or death. Being Black means turning the other cheek when a punch in the face is due. Being Black is fear and love and fearing love all at once. But it isn't always a daunting thing to be Black.

To be Black also means being so cool and suave that everybody wants to look, walk, talk, move, and sing like you. To be Black means you have a natural talent for greatness in ANYTHING you find is your passion. To be Black is to let your thick hair reach outward like a sunburst behind your head. To be Black is to easily connect to the Source of all creation. To be Black is to be an embodiment of trendsetting creativity. It is to be influence itself. To be Black is to be best friends with the elements. To be Black is to be envied and even feared. To be Black is to be the majority. To be Black is to dominate the gene pool. To be Black is to have the power to make or break any system and to be resilient. To be Black is to share knowledge, to tell stories, and to be the home from which all things have come. These things are what it means to be Black, Queenie.

Life between Blackness and Feminism is a unique one, but in the end, it is all about balance. When you have an imbalance, you have inequality. Humans are the only species that defy the laws of nature just because they can, but the laws are there to keep order and maintain harmony. Lionesses typically do not fight Lions; they know their place in the pride and have found peace with their roles. Bucks do not go shaving off their horns to try to be a doe. They live life the way they naturally were created. Keep your purpose in mind and fill the roles you need to fill as necessary. In one moment, your role may be to follow while in the next moment, you are to lead. Remember, you have the wisdom to determine the difference. In the same vein of living a purpose-driven life, note that your "tribe" will come with its own movements. When it comes to race, there will be many movements to support, but when it comes to sex, you'll be faced with one question: Am I a feminist?

As my younger self, I must inform you of my take away from the feminists of today. Their movement has come to suggest to me that women can AND MUST do what men do. That is not how it started. If I am not mistaken, the feminist movement came about because some intelligent woman said, "Hold up. Behind every great man is a woman. Why are you treating me like property instead of your queen?" Having equal access to money, business, education, and property, and having the right to vote are notions I can stand behind. However, changing the narrative to "Women should do everything for themselves because men are obsolete!" is a ridiculous and irrationally fashioned concept.

Perhaps the focus on the feminine is a long, drawn out destined response to the patriarchal society in America that aimed to stifle Feminine Power for so many years. Either way, with all of its good and not-so-good elements, the feminist movement has developed over time into a gift and a curse. The deeply skewed view of independence for women should call into review what this disproportion may mean for family values, especially for Black families. There are already systems in place to break up the family dynamics and attack Black men. The welfare system, for example, made it imperative to nurture the idea of a single, independent woman. With this in mind, it does not take rocket science or religion to see how feminism has transformed into a societal fad that celebrates the deprivation of male roles and identity. Confusion and imbalance has come from modern day feminism and has, in turn, helped to break the basics of family dynamics.

Family should be important to you, Queenie, because that is your legacy. Protecting your tribe is protecting your legacy, so be very careful to whom you are loyal. Not all blood is your family and not all family is blood. Choose your inner circle the way you would choose your future mate. You are Woman, yes. You are Black, yes. Although it is helpful to know which side you will take, should you ever need to choose one over the other, remember that you are everything. Knowing when to be one way or the other is key when dealing with your immediate and global family. Master it. That is what being Black and Woman is about.

Being Black and Woman is being bold. It's commanding the space you hold and having the audacity to claim it loud and clear with elegance and poise. It's having the range to be "ethnic" and "high-class" like there's no difference between the two. It's walking in your truth and refusing to apologize for it. It's being emotional and vulnerable and not being afraid to show it. It's birthing nations, training up valiant children, owning profitable businesses, and still being an awesome wife and mother. It's taking on your role in your families, personal and otherwise, and working it because that's just what you do. It looks like running the world in front of and behind the curtains. It looks like wealth, nice cars, and cigars on Saturday and chicken dinner plates from Miss Mable down at the church on Sunday. It's supporting Black business, Black women, Black men, Black children, and everything else Black. It's pouring love into the Black community with your child care, baked goods, credit services, clothing line, or hair salon. Being Black and Woman is celebrating the next woman's beauty and glory while acknowledging your own. Being Black and Woman is more wonderful than not.

Now, Queenie, I must leave you with some advice. Know who you are by way of observation, meditation, and prayer. Results mirror your alignment to your purpose and are congruent with your choices and your indecision. Know your history in this land. Understand how you, the Black Woman, directly affects economics, culture, and politics, and use that to your advantage. Refrain from entertaining dubious minds and manufactured public opinions of the Black Woman, for you will find they inaccurately portray you. Always use your powers for good, aim to be of service through inspiration with truth, and, by the way, you are beautiful. Treat yourself like you would a superstar; your light can shine just as bright if you let it.

You'll be blessed, young Queenie.

Love,
Queen Ex

RECOMMENCER

by Linda Ferguson

Ah, dear friend, a new task for you —
an unexpected journey —
lace up your thick boots and bring along
a peach, some bandages, a shovel, a seed.
Also, bring that nubby knitted hat
you wore all winter — remember
how it made you laugh? — and of course
you'll need your new heart too,
that hard green pear,
already bruised.
Dear friend, you're pale —
it's alright — go ahead and bring
your fear as well — without it,
you're not fully you. Come,
feel the soles of your feet pressing
against the earth — it takes your weight,
you take up space — see,
you are slowly moving and you have
everything you need.

LETTER TO MY TEENAGE SELF

by Nikki Marrone

Sometimes I miss the wildness of my teenage years - breaking into abandoned buildings, climbing trees, staying out for days, and picking up outfits and bruises on the way. Everything was wonderful and terrible, and everyone was always madly in love or completely heartbroken. When I look back at that time it's with a mixture of nostalgia and terror. There's a part of me that's in awe of that girl, her total disregard for self-preservation, how she could run at the world headfirst, eyes closed, with no care for the consequences. It's with that same awe that I look at teenage girls now. You don't realize how powerful you really are, how capable of change and how much further along in life you are from the generation above you. But on the other hand, I want to go back and hold the teenage me in my arms. I want to tell her that's it's ok, she's ok. That she doesn't have to work so hard, and these days will be over soon. That she doesn't have to be this person if that person doesn't feel right.

Although I admire it in a seasick way, a lot of my bravery in my teens came from a place of self-loathing. I was able to push boundaries and take chances because I wasn't very fussed about whether I came back alive. Oblivion was usually the goal. I don't know if it was because of societal pressure, or the highly inappropriate and unwanted attention from men far too old, or a genetic predisposition to bad mental health and anxiety, but somewhere along the line I had learned that I was wrong, that I was not good enough, not smart enough, not thin enough. I was so angry with myself all the time. How that happened, I don't know – I am still trying to understand what makes young women go to war with themselves. But the judgement choir never stopped singing. It still sings now, though not as loudly or as often, and when it does, I try not to self-medicate with straight vodka or starvation.

As I entered into my twenties, I found myself fitting into my skin more. Thanks to my art I was surrounded by well-rounded women who weren't afraid to be themselves, no topic was taboo and they stood on stage and roared like lions. I learned to grab my passion and run with it, to shout about the things I cared about and to approach situations with kindness and respect. I realized that the women I wanted so badly to be as a teenager were actually my first female crushes. I realized that I didn't have to let people treat me however they wanted, and that I could put up healthy boundaries to protect myself. Without these women I think I would have stayed on the path of self-destruction and believed that suffering was what made me creative and gave me value. To these women I owe everything, and the biggest advice I would give to my younger self and others is to find those role models, whether that be in person or in the media. I have learned that when you give a group of women a safe space in which to be open, something truly special occurs.

It was strange to let go of all that mess, and for a long time I grieved for it. Partying was, I felt, a defining feature of my personality. I was the life and soul of the party and everyone wanted to come along for the ride. But the new-found thrill of leaving somewhere with all my belongings, having not been felt up by someone inappropriate, has still not left me. This is not to say that I have it all figured out – I am not a beacon of sanity. If you have denied yourself nourishment, you can often deny yourself emotional nourishment, too. I find it hard to accept love, hard to accept stability. A large capacity for joy means an even larger capacity for gloom. Self-harm is a shape shifter, but I'm working on it. And the more honest I am, the happier I become. I don't believe in self-destruction as a means to creativity any more. And the less preoccupied I am with what I look like, or what I did last night, the more energy I have to give to my work. I managed to be successful despite my demons, not because of them.

I often wonder if my young self would be horrified at my Friday nights now: eating pasta and watching TV with someone who is nice to me. Would she think me mundane? But the truth of it is that most of the friends that I drank with have had to stop. They wash up one by one like driftwood, and we stand together on the shore in shocked relief. We cook, we talk, we work. People have started having children and going to bed early. And all the boring "grown-upness" that we rejected then now seems somehow rebellious. It is an act of rebellion to remain present, to go against society's desire for you to numb yourself, to look away. But we must not look away. I think the younger me would be proud of the woman I have grown into, the same way that I am proud to see the young women around me coming into their own. We often put too much pressure on the next generation to save us, but I grew up without the conversations around feminism, sexuality, and what it meant to be women. It took decades for me to find my voice. The lesson I want to pass onto my daughter and all the others is that she was born with that voice, and that there is always a space for her. She is good enough, and nobody defines her but herself. At this time in our history, it has never been more pressing to have as many voices singing as we can.

THOUGHTS FOR A FRIEND AT 4 A.M.

by Linda Ferguson

It is time for you
to go,
time for you
to take up the pickaxe
and swing,
to find the gold
buried beneath your feet,
to find the voice
in your bones
that repeats:
you are strong
you are fine
you can sing.
Go ahead —
release
your grip
and approach
the green mountain,
keep reaching
for the next root,
the next rock

until you work
your way to the top,
then stop and open your breath
to the ocean below,
see how it surges,
moving sand, boats,
human beings.
Look up and see
the extended bodies
of birds trusting
the force of air
pressed to their wings,
and know
that you, too, can move,
that the pull of the moon
is not floating in space
but generating
within the glorious stretch
of your own wings.
Bend your knees
and feel your body, rising,
feel the air beneath the soles
of your feet,
feel the charging
of your heartbeat,
and relish
your terror,
your ecstasy!

FOUR WORDS TO YOUR 17 YEAR OLD SELF

by Eve Lyons

A found poem written by friends on Facebook

Please brush your teeth
You can do it
Love yourself more, please
I say fuck 'em
Do a breast self-exam
There's lots of time
Be nicer to parents
You're gay! Be happy
You will surprise yourself
You are ok really
Buy stock in Microsoft
Be true to yourself
You are my hero
You will survive this
Success teaches you nothing
Get your degree early
You don't have to
Maybe you deserve more
Are you kidding me!?
Be a better friend
Follow your passion NOW
You will do fine.

LOVE, AMANDA

by Amanda Jess

Dear Teenage Self,

This will be difficult to swallow, but it's important you hear it. That person you feel is your entire world, who leaves you gasping for air each time they walk out of your life? One day, they won't be in it anymore. I know it's going to be hard for you to accept because they seem like the most important person in your life right now and you don't believe you can get over them. They're not, and you can.

In fact, you are the most important person in your life, and that relationship is hurting you. No amount of waiting is going to make them become the person you want them to be. Sometimes you catch glimpses of the thoughtful, fun, affectionate partner you want, and you convince yourself the good outweighs the bad. A handwritten note and a hug in the hallway can't make up for how many times you find yourself questioning your worth after they dump you, yet again.

Don't stay because you're worried about breaking their heart; you need to look after yourself. When it's over, don't answer the phone when they call. Don't talk to them at school. Don't email them. You can't be their friend.

You probably don't believe me yet that that's what is best for you. Let me try to convince you.

First, let's start with consent. Imagine you're kissing someone and it's getting heated. They're pulling you closer, your heart is racing, their hands begin to move around your body–but before they try to take it further, they stop. "Are you up for this?" they ask. You're so into them, but you're not ready. "Let's just make out, ok?" And it is ok. They smile and you resume. The two of you have a discussion later about what you're ready to do together. There's no pressure, just an open dialogue. Both of you make it clear you'll let each other know when you're ready to take the next step.

You could have this. You should have this. Consent is not coercive. There shouldn't be hesitation, silence, or the word "no" being ignored as one person goes ahead anyway. You should feel respected and safe.

You know that feeling you have when they keep asking for things you're not sure you're ready to do? Where you're uncomfortable, but you push it down because they're your partner and in relationships, you compromise? That's not the kind of compromise you should ever have to make.

Let's also talk about communication. Sometimes you or your partner are going to be upset and you may want to have a conversation about that. You should, privately. It's not okay for someone to yell at you in front of your peers, no matter how upset they are. It's not okay for them to keep going as tears roll down your face, your face turns several shades of red, and everyone around you tells them to leave you alone.

You should both be open to hearing how the other person feels at an appropriate time and place, and you shouldn't have to fear you'll lose them by talking about it. Sometimes you'll realize it's not going to get better. Trust this instinct.

It can be difficult to not get swept up in it all, to become so intertwined with who you think is your person that you begin to lose yourself. It's human to crave that closeness, to desire intimacy, to feel a connection. Don't stop looking for that. I want you to know, though, that romantic love isn't the only kind of love. You matter, regardless of your relationship status.

You tend to see the good in every person. Never lose this. People will disappoint you; that's inevitable. Sometimes you'll set your expectations too high and other times, people won't be who you thought they were. It's okay to be sad when this happens, but don't lose faith in humanity. You can keep believing in people while also being kind to yourself. You aren't obligated to stay in a situation that hurts you because the other person is hurting, too. You'll take a long time to learn this lesson because of how much you care about people. That's a great quality to have; just make sure you care for you, too.

I know boys have compared you to other girls and you do it yourself, but they are not your competition. Don't let anyone pit you against other women. You will meet so many women who will inspire you, who will cheer you on for your accomplishments big and small, who will show up for you and quietly sit beside you while you deal with loss and anger.

Know that you are enough. Those who truly love you will support you in your growth as a person, but they won't push you to be or look like somebody else. Know that you are not responsible for anyone else's happiness. You can and should support people, but not at the expense of your own well-being.

Know your partner's anger is not your fault and you can't bear the burden of helping them deal with it by yourself. Know that you have people in your life who will help you leave this relationship. Know that you're doing the right thing. Know that you are loved, and you will love again.

Love,
Amanda

CRUSHING

by Katrina Mundy

I stared at Jason
every day.
8th grade
Jason
with long swirls of
big black curls
and dark chocolate
brown eyes
framed by lashes
that always looked wet.
I must have been drawn
to sadness.

Those eyes looking
eagerly everywhere
except
in my direction.
Gangly blonde
untamed cowlick
my narrow shoulders
attempting to fold their way
into my stomach
like a football note
and eyes that looked
either to the floor
or at him.
Jason.

Gangly wasn't fatal.
It wasn't,
but I should probably tell you

I had to wear a mouth guard
in preparation for braces;
like a boxer wears.

Believe me
I felt the punch
of thick plastic
my lips attempting to curl
their way around its absurd
protrusion of both my
top teeth
and bottom.

Can I trust you
with the worst part?

This mouth guard
ill fitting and awkward
as it was,
as I was,
I used my mouth
as a dam
and stayed silent
to hide the monstrosity.

But in my attempt
to protect myself and maintain order
the result was a natural disaster
building —
a collection of saliva
coming from all areas of my mouth
held captive by the guards
only emphasized
by nerves
and long hours
collecting.
pooling.
marinating.

Jason
one fateful day
sat in front of me in math,
and I was

happy
just to rest my dreamy teenage eyes
on the back of his head
until
he started to turn around
and everything
slowed.
down.
too.
slow.
And he opened his beautiful mouth
while looking me in the eyes.
I thought I might shatter
into tiny pieces of glass
and he said,
"Hey. You got a pencil?"

And at that moment
when he met my eyes
and asked a favor
of me
of
me
couldn't help
but smile.

And when I did,
the guards
abandoned me
stepped aside
and a ~~stream~~
a ~~river~~
a waterfall
spilled
gushed
and fell out of my mouth
onto my desk.

And still not horrified yet
in slow motion
as a reflex
I attempted to contain
all the still flowing fountain

in all its glory
with both hands
and tried
to rescue it
back into my mouth
with a sound only similar
to someone slurping soup
so loudly in a library
that people would have to
stop what they were doing
crane necks and turn,
look at the soup slurper appalled,
and remove the offender at once.

I saw his face turn
from relaxed
to disgusted
and my face
burned heavy
with a burden
only a crushed teenager
would understand.

But now
at 47
how lucky am I
to have believed I felt love
to have drooled over a boy
and today write
and laugh
and laugh
while I unpack old burdens
that no longer hold weight.

DEAR FUTURE SELF

by Isabella Sanchez

Dear Future Self,

Hello! It is your sixteen (almost seventeen) year-old self! I am writing this letter to you in order to document the life lessons I have learned so far. Also, I hope I have overcome the goals I detail later in this letter (that I am actually writing on a whim). I am spontaneously writing this to you after my second week of my senior year of high school. So far, it has been a series of ups and downs. Even though it's only been a mere fourteen days, a lot has happened... And I am *not* overexaggerating this time, however that is not what this letter is about. This summer has allowed me the ability to discover who I truly am and who I desire to be in the future, future me... and I hope that these two goals that I detail for myself and the future are occuring in your world, not only for you, but for others around you.

Number One. I have made it my number one goal to love myself and radiate positivity. I know I have struggled in these areas (one more than the other, which you know), but I have realized that in this day and age, nobody is perfect so you might as well love yourself. This mind, this spirit, this body... *I was given who I am for a reason.* Although I am surrounded by a world filled with celebrities with these abnormally gorgeous outer appearances and perfectly laid out lives, I *know* that their lives are not all "rainbows and butterflies," but that they experience the same insecurities that I do. Also, these factors should not be the most significant worries in my life. Being "beautiful" is not the most important detail in your life. You should not be focusing on your physical appearances, but pursuing genuine, unconditional relationships and a life with *a purpose*. I know that it's overplayed like a broken record, but do not shy away from **being kind**. People today need a reassuring smile and source of positivity due to all the negativity our atmosphere contains. Be **that** girl who *smiles* at strangers on the street, *gives* a compliment, and *understands* the world. We need more positivity in our lives and once you let it in, you can impact someone's day for the greater good. **Disregard** the jealousy and hatred in your life. **Fill your life with positivity and joy!** You will be much happier. The weights on your shoulders will be lifted once you allow this positivity in your life! I hope that you become a positive and optimistic role model for those around you. Moreover, that when you read this, society has changed the idea that being "perfect" and "beautiful" is our number one goal, because, especially as a young teenager, this should be something I do not have to worry about this much.

Number Two. I hope that you have embraced who you are, no matter what society or your family and friends say. Society today tells me that if I want to wear a skirt four inches above the knee, then I am "asking for attention." However, if I wear a skirt four inches below the knee, I am a prude. I can't go out of the house without "cleaning myself up," yet I can't go out of the house with too much makeup, because then I will look like I "tried too hard." They tell us that we *can't* be tough, funny, strong, and in charge. This list extends upon every aspect of a female's life, and you should **NOT** give into them. We are all beautiful in our *own* ways. **NOBODY**, whether it is society, social media, or people in your life, should tell you who you are. Your body was made for your own satisfaction, not others. You are not lesser than if you do not choose to be with a man. You can handle life on your own. Be independent. Love yourself. Wear that funky shirt you saw online. You can choose who you want to be, but you have to overcome these strict, unnecessary regulations that society and the people around you expect you to abide by. Do not be afraid to wear what you want and be who you want. YOU WERE GIVEN ONE LIFE! Cherish it and live the life you, and only you, desire. Do not worry about what others think, because in the end, it's just you and who **YOU** perceive yourself as.

I hope you have taken away some key points from these two aspirations of mine. I hope you are continuing to practice and learn from them everyday. I hope you are still trying to achieve these goals of mine… or better yet, have overcome them! Just do what makes you truly happy and everything will be alright. See you on the flip side!

Sending my love,
Your Teenage Self

Not Your Bag

by Kate Autumn Bokoles

I have to tell you something…

You don't need to worry about what you look like: Short hair, long hair. Smooth, unsmooth. Dark hair, blonde hair, grey hair, coarse hair. Thin. Fat. Loose skin, taut skin, wrinkles. Long legs, short legs. Curves. Flat. Crooked. Symmetrical. White teeth, teeth stained with the love of coffee. Stomach. Butt. Skin. Sag. Chins. Neck. Bust. Hips. Stomach again.

You don't need to worry about any of this.

A long time ago somebody handed you a bag, and you don't have to carry it any longer.

Someone tried to hobble you because they were afraid of your power.

You have too much to do here to be slowed down by extra baggage.

Put it
down.

It doesn't belong to
you.

It's
time.

It's time to get things
done.

SEXUALITY, SELF IMAGE, AND #METOO

IN PRAISE OF THICK THIGHS

by Aruni Wijesinghe

She rubs her thighs
together, bow against
bow, quivering the strings
of a primal call. Thick
thighs are a portal to an
inner universe.

rounded thighs rubbed with
sandalwood paste, ample like
feast days, tabletop enough to
hold pitchers of yogurt, bowls
of butter

sacred thighs, the pillars of
the temple where we come
to worship, prostrate
ourselves on the altar of
plenty, gorge ourselves on
flesh and enlightenment

thick thighs, two columns uphold the
pelvic bowl where we come to burn
offerings of animal fat and incense
phalanx of thick-thigh'd girls adorn
the temple frieze, provokes
cellulite-fueled paroxysms of ecstasy

Devotees of the Cult of
Thick sway and faint,
enraptured by the applause
of thick thighs running up

the temple stairs.
stilled thighs buttress the sanctuary
walls priestess swoons over the
 fumes, predicting the razing of cities,
the fall of empires

fevered thighs vibrate with the
primordial pulse friction kindles
fire, catches the tinder of a
nation's drowsing amygdala

Thick thighs are made to
withstand the long climb uphill
to unseat emperors, topple
rawboned deities.

LETTERS TO MEN

by Kate Autumn Bokoles

To the Man Who Had Never Seen So Much Hair:

A decade after I offered you my naked body, years after I stopped re-turning your calls, there are still hairs that I pluck because of you.

I had thought (at the time) that when people chose to become naked with each other, they were choosing to become intimate with the quirky bits, the parts that were not groomed and made presentable for the world, the mystery underneath. I thought that's what sex meant. A disrobing. A sharing of the truth. I thought it meant no longer needing to cover the animal or the wild.

But with a few concise words (you were always so concise, I loved that about you) you disrobed me of that idea. And I was shocked. My animal body shut down and hid itself away. I wanted so desperately to share my nakedness with you but from that day forward I could never figure out how.

Of course, my body was the wise one after all. It took me so many years of shame and efforting to realize what anyone could have seen from the beginning. There was no way to share myself with you at all.

Dear Mr. Doctor:

I was 18 years old and I had heard what happened to 18 year old girls at the doctor so I prepared myself for you. I was going to take control of my body. I was going to say No. You walked in and said "Take off your panties" and I did. I did. (Turns out I wasn't prepared after all.) The pain was, of course, excruciating, and so was the shame of my betrayal. I didn't cry out. I didn't ask you to stop (Why would I? I had never asked you to start in the first place.) When you finally noticed how much pain I was in you did stop, but couldn't help making sure I knew who had the power here. You couldn't help yourself from standing over me with the object you had shoved inside me and saying, "I'll stop but if you become sexually active you'll be right back here on this table." Maybe those weren't quite your words, but I could read through the lines even then.

You, my childhood doctor, were the first one to penetrate me. It goes without saying that you did so without consent.

Dear one-time client who laid down on my treatment table and told me I was beautiful and tried to force me into a hug after the session:

Please stop.

Dear Mr. Teacher:

You've known me since I was 9 years old, tiny and precocious. I used to run up to you on the playground when I was 10, 11, 12 years old, fling myself down on the grass with my feet in the air, you would grab me by the ankles and throw me into the sky so that I landed on my feet, having flipped completely around. You understood my need to fly.

When I was 13 you grabbed my hips instead, your touch intimate and casual. I was small even then, so the breadth of your hands touched all the bony landmarks of my pelvis, pubis to sacrum. I was standing at the front of the classroom, the rest of the students quietly working, your touch so brief it was hard to think of it in terms of assault.

After all, we all knew the girls you preferred and I wasn't one of them.

Still, I remember what it was like to be a girl who had never been touched like that. I remember what it was like to suddenly be a girl who had been touched like that. And I had only gone up to your desk to ask you for a paperclip.

Dear Barely Pubescent Boy who touched the place where my breast began and my rib cage ended:

I know it's hard to be small and just barely pubescent in a world of teenage boys, but my body wasn't on offer for you to milk for some social leverage. It's tempting to dismiss this attempt to impress the locker room

104

boys since it was so…banal and, well, pathetic. And in the scheme of things, so much less damaging than what was in store for me once I got out into the real world of men. After all, to boast that you had touched my breast was stretching it just a bit, don't you think? Yet in the interest of beginnings, in the interest of tracing back to the roots of a thing, let us not step over the fact that this was the first time my body was used as an object for a man to feel more like a man. You, Teenage Boy, introduced me to that particular kind of internal confusion that has become all too familiar: letting a man touch me because he was pretending he wasn't doing it in the first place. How do you say No to something if the whole thing is buried beneath a veneer of plausible deniability?

It turns out you still can, but I didn't know that at the time.

Dear Colleague:

After the fall out, after I moved my business out of your office (because that's how it goes in the workplace, a woman either puts up with it with fake nervous giggles that you refuse to notice, or she upends her life to avoid you), what stays with me is the look on your face when I said that women don't need you to compliment them. That mirrors are everywhere and our beauty is sitting there, inarguable. You're not a commodity. You're not the missing link, as if we suffer some strange disease of partial blindness that requires us to depend on the men around us to say if we are beautiful or not. (Spoiler: we are.)

You looked so shocked. Sometimes I allow myself the fantasy that that blew your mind a little. That it shook loose some complacency. That maybe you could see yourself in the mirror after that conversation. Although, let's be real. That's pretty optimistic on my part.

Your heart, your soul, your mind matter greatly in this world (even yours, my not-so-favorite-person, even yours), but your opinion about me matters not at all. Except for that tiny wrinkle about having to move my business away from you in order to find a safe place for myself and my female clients. In that case, your opinion ended up mattering quite a lot.

To the both of you:

You both stood there leaning against the case after class, two men who loomed large in my life. I hovered along the edge as I do, while you bantered, like you do. I was enamored with your strength, your height, your mass, and your lack of self-doubt. And then you made a joke that I'd never heard before but surely you both had heard so many times, you laughed like all the old boys do. The ones with no self-doubt. It blew my mind.

I'll say now what I didn't say then: You cannot attack the body of a woman and then pretend that you do not hate all that a woman stands for. Everyone loves a woman "in her place" (the place that men have placed her for safekeeping). That's not worth talking about. Let the record show now, do you love a woman in her place: her body, her nature, that which is outside of your control or your ken… even if she scares you?

I ask this question now, from this distance of space and time because back then you always thought that I was so adorable when I was angry. I am small and in the end we all must admit that I was not worth much weight in your eyes. Much like that joke that you told each other in your back-slapping camaraderie.

I'm taking the only kind of weight that I can, the weight of distance, words on page where I control the narrative, where your superior height and depth of voice can't drown out my own.

Where you aren't even listening at all.

DEFINE BICURIOUS

by Amon Elise

"Amon, stop playing around. You're no lesbian."

This is from a mother who told me she'd love me regardless of who I am or what I choose to do. This is after the seventh time I've told her. This is with the illusion of hilarity that I try to force feed my mother a dose of me.

When I was younger, below four feet and therefore not allowed to speak with the grown folks, I ran off to the back room with a girl my age. Giggly and cautious, underneath a yellowed comforter my little fingers roamed free. Under the cover, we played and kissed and grabbed and squeezed, underneath where we wouldn't be heard, nor seen.

How do you tell your best friend the reason why you dumped him in freshman year is strictly because you were bored with this game? That you love him, but on a deeper side that goes so far beyond the physical, lips will never form the feelings into meaning? He looked at me with tears as he told me how we could've made it. And I lied to him when I said we could've. How can forever start with secrets? With someone you truly don't know? He'll never believe me when I tell him, but I have a feeling he's known the longest of all.

I'm sixteen when I realize I've developed a crush on my cousin's lover. It's moved past a desire to map her curves, and into uncharted areas. Innocent, for I would never touch her, but I fully understand why my cousin loves her. My imagination runs wild. Dates, discussions over books, movies, eating at new places, meeting new faces. The idea of someone just like her by my side is enough to make me eager, if only to please her.

In high school, I shared a secret for a want of a kiss - with the first girl friend I managed to get close to. She shared the same interest, as she was supposed to. Before I got the courage to ask her to try with me, she said she already tried it with another girl. One I never got a chance to be.

At twelve, the family reunion I just couldn't miss had holed me up in the living room. Everyone else was outside, eating pie, pre-made kool-aid popsicles and greens. From the kitchen, in a shield of hopeful solitude, the elderly whisper of my cousin's transgressions. "If my lord only knew how to change her, she might go to heaven one day," declared my grandmother, leader of the pack. She wore her smile like a uniform when she kissed that same cousin goodbye mere hours later.

My brother and I sit poolside, content to idolize the relatively short span of our lifetimes. Our toes dip into the shallow end, causing ripples to spread in precise directions. Mid-banter, I mention the possibility that I may find support and tranquility within the arms of woman. My brother's response: "Bullshit."

By the time I enter my senior year, I've finally figured it out that I don't collect friends. I have a flock. Made of those too weak to tell me they love me, willing to prostrate themselves for my platonic side, and of those strong enough to look me in the eye and deal with my bitter sarcasm, seeing right through me. One such friend, a best friend and thus the latter, now tells me, "You're on the fence. Go on ahead and fall if you want to, but while you're up there, enjoy the view."

I date boys. Eventually men as I grow older, a little bit bolder with my trysts. Perceived to be strictly dickly, my lascivious - and thus infamous - nature precedes me even before I meet people. My badge of honor, so at least my mother can be certain (because she'll never be proud) of her daughter.

The end of sixth grade, my mother approaches me between the pages of a harlequin. Interrupting the example of how I am supposed to be. As long as I read books like these, instead of Zane's fantasies, I'll be safe from her "advice." Yet, today she approaches me and asks me the fatal question: "Amon, do boys interest you? I don't see you with any."

"Sometimes, I just get bored after a while."

I tell her the truth by omission.

I've become a sexual predator. An hour of sinless peace is unattainable. The audacity of my thoughts captures my attention. I'm devoted beyond mention, lost, and fixated around several thoughts rotating under a single idea. Under her? I want to give her an ocean, watching the waves roll, strolling over her. Lifting her to heights I've never been able to reach, the goal to be uncontested by the next one. But as much as I fiend, all I've ever been is a host to the dream.

My favorite cousin, the lawyer, and her curvy milk-skinned girlfriend pull me aside one day. Before I even start, they tell me what I apparently already show. A walk around the park allows me to ask everything I've ever wanted to know. A community spun from the forever shunned. And I now have a key to this city.

Flashbacks constantly plague me, bits and pieces of a picture so vague, but insistent enough to invade me. Even now, swift enough to evade me. It holds the evidence of another time, another place, maybe around ten, at a sleepover – at a friend's. My panties are a puddle on the floor. There is a solid, hairy leg that I climb into an unknown bed to reach and hands with five thick fingers each. I thank my mind for erasing, even replacing whatever follows – my memories only go so deep. To tell a soul would give my (grand)mother an excuse for the secret I keep, and I refuse to let my sense of self be shattered when she lays it at my feet.

Eight-teen: A boyfriend, trying to make me laugh after I share my vacillation, announces, "Amon, you're a lesbian with an addiction to penis." I have been defined by the smiling eyes of the puppet I have chosen to role play with for the time being. His days are now numbered, our paths as divergent as perpendicular lines.

Shopping for homecoming dresses, my next girl friend at the time dragged me into her dressing room. Insisting I pull up and adjust her zipper. I do, but I take my time. As I leave, I notice that my dressing room "is now occupied", and she offers the bright idea to share hers. As she changes in front of me I'm officially condemned, frozen in my own whirlwind, as my eyes consume every inch. She has the nerve to blush after our eyes meet in the mirror, and this empowers me to touch and feel wherever I can, and she lets me. Victory, as always, goes to the spider and our dates outside are none the wiser.

I am unable to reach nirvana, because those holding double-x chromosomes need not apply. I would be forced to bend over a man unworthy of deserving me if I sheltered within the robes of Islam. An abomination is how I am defined by the Christian nation. And they wonder why I retreat?! The punishments for who I am I refuse to repeat. I thank the lonely entity that approves of me – She is of my own invention. Her only intention is to love – and love hard. We adapt codes and rituals of the esoteric, and at our choosing. The bigger picture isn't as exclusive as one would think.

Men usually become playthings, fling after fling, coaching me into an otherworldly being. Slaughter and move on, developing a pattern of blissful ignorance of broken hearts I left behind. I could date one, and he wouldn't even know how much it would hurt when he would date another. Maybe the girl I've been crushing on for a year now. Who cares anyway? Apathy, now tattooed on my chest, and I could care less - regardless, for me, there would be no life after death.

To this day, my lips go unkissed, missed, by those I want to enlist on my team. In all honesty, I wouldn't know what to do with a woman if I got the opportunity. Could I even acknowledge, let alone satisfy her needs? Could I get over the fact that it, like mine, bleeds? I feel I'll never reach a stage so freed.

As disrespectful as it was, my friends and I enjoyed making fun of our veiled friend back in freshman year. Cloaked and shielded to hide her form, at any slight exposure we would swoon. A wrist, an ear, an ankle would cause us to drift bits of slightly erotic poetry her way and she would laugh and forgive us. Even when a lock of hair could send us into an uproar. Later, with age and intersectional feminism on my tongue, I would ask for forgiveness. Her response, "Please, Amon – if you were serious I'd know it. You're no lesbian - that would be obvious. If you were to tell me that right now, I'd find it so funny I'd die. They're all just a bunch of confused nymphos anyway." The laugh I imitated sounded like my mother's.

SWINGING BOTH WAYS

by Nikki Marrone

You told me I had to choose.
One or the other.
You said it was black or white, that I couldn't be both;
I said a pendulum swings both ways in equal force coming to rest in
perfect equilibrium.
You said I had better start making sense —
It's me or her.
Hetero or homo? You decide.
I said let's start with semantics;
Homo takes me back to classroom giggles and playground bullies,
the word followed by finger points and a sad faced boy
whose only crime was to colour his shoelaces pink.
I remember the teacher taking that same sad faced boy and turning it
all around.
He said homo means man —
a whole species walking tall on two legs,
proud and strong they took the earth.
And Hetero it means different —
It means other.
That proves nothing you argue.
So let's move onto science -
Sexuality is a spectrum.
Flowing from the source it drifts down the stream, expanding to an ocean.
Now social bias is a factor and the need to reproduce creates attraction.
But not everyone needs a baby to feel complete,
and those who do, have enough love to care for another's child,
or have their own regardless.
It's not natural he moans.
Moving onto nature —
Did you know that deep sea squid mates with both
and that proud lions practice polygamy?

From the age of ten to the time they mate the bottlenose dolphin is gay.
Gentleman penguins love one another and our cousins the chimps
swing either way.
Let's finish with attraction —
Your arms around me make me safe with rough hands from a long day
of labour,
the way they graze my skin so strangely familiar —
There's no denying the chemistry there.
But her softness, bright eyes and gentle caresses,
hourglass curves so easy to trace,
well she also caught my eye.
We sit in silence and reflect on all that's said,
I wonder how I had never known,
how long this realisation was to come.
All the worry and all the shame.
He concludes with a resounding "I don't like it."
"Thank you", I smile and nod my head.
You have pushed the pendulum and now it's free to swing both ways
coming to rest in perfect equilibrium.

How it Feels to Have a Sexual Predator on the Supreme Court

by Eve Lyons

When I hear about a Great White Shark
attacking someone on Cape Cod
my first thought is always
what did he do to provoke the shark?
Is this why so many people's first response
when hearing a woman was raped
is to ask *what was she wearing?*
Or *was she drunk?*

Anita Hill followed Clarence Thomas to her second job
Though years later she told white men in the Senate
about his lewd comments and groping
If you were sexually harassed, they said, *why did you follow him?*

Shira says that on her first date with her husband
she didn't want to have sex, but he went ahead anyway.
He didn't even use a condom.
Still, she doesn't call it rape.
A decade and one child later,
they are getting divorced.
Maybe that's why I never wanted to have sex, she tells me.

Katherine and I are driving and listening to a podcast
A woman recalls thinking *at least I'm not being murdered*
while having sex with her lover.

Katherine confesses to me that her first husband
raped her every time they had sex.
She had to lie to convince her family, herself
it was okay to leave.

When Donald Trump was elected president
so many people asked *how this could happen*
while in therapists' offices women confided
he seemed familiar.
He was the husband, the father,
the uncle, the neighbor, the pastor
they had known all their lives.
They'd come to accept this was how men were:
Boys will be boys.

11,417 sharks are killed by humans every hour
while 82 sharks per year kill some unlucky swimmer.
The shark was here first.
The shark doesn't come with cruise ships and spears.
The shark is just trying to survive.

Three decades after Anita Hill
women are starting to say
Me too.
Another sexual predator is seated
on the Supreme Court.
The men are asking the same questions.

But women are asking
Why should boys be like this?
Should we let men be like this?
How did we let it go this long?
How can we leave?

*Previously published in the *Prachya Review*.

#BODYGOALS

by Aisha Hussain

To the girl who tells me she loves my body and wants my body:
I too want my body
I want to love my body the way you love it
the way I wish my mother taught me to love it
the way I wish I loved it before I was a size 4
the way I wish I loved it before I could do a push-up

I want to turn back the clock
and take back the social conditioning that I MUST have
looooooong, toned legs
boobs more than a mouthful. perky.
petite torso, slightly chiseled abdomen
(but not more defined than my male counterpart)
and an ass that makes zipping my size 4 jeans a full-time job

Father capitalism forgive me for I have sinned
and kept the receipts for all the things you made me think I needed to buy
to make myself into something I am not
to help me disappear just enough to make them notice
I want a refund on time spent wondering how I can hide my body
contemplating how small I can make myself

I want to rinse the hate off my body
and scrub away the comments from men who told me to workout
to lose a few but keep the fat ass
I want to unlearn that chubby is undesirable
to peel away the years of body dysmorphia
of cringing at my rolls
and wishing myself into a smaller size
To the girl who says I am body goals
I need you to see me fighting alongisde you,

reclaiming every inch, bump, roll, & ingrown hair
I was taught to be ashamed of
tirelessly working to repot, plant, and soil the woman I imagined being
before they told me I was too much of this and not enough of that

To the girl who tells me she loves my body and wants my body:
I need you to remember
everything they want you to be is only a fraction of all that you are

BARE IT ALL

by Jennifer Furner

A tall woman in a black track suit was assigned to show us around the health club. My husband and I followed her and nodded as she pointed out the different areas of the complex. When we arrived at the locker room entrance, my husband went left into the men's alone, and I went to the right with the staff person into the women's. I was immediately confronted with bare boobs and bodies of all shapes and sizes.

The staff woman told me about the towel service and the sauna, but I couldn't hear her over all the nakedness. No one seemed to notice that I was standing there completely dressed from head to toe. They moved around before me, talking and laughing and trying to get ready, not paying any mind to their own nudity or each other's. I felt as if I were a spectator at a zoo, watching strange creatures behind glass. It's as if they didn't realize they were indeed naked.

And then I felt a little offended. I could understand if these women are comfortable exposing themselves to each other — they're all part of the same gym and this is normal for them — but shouldn't they cover up when "company" comes by? Shouldn't they be a little embarrassed that they've been caught? Shouldn't they feel a little ashamed?

Because that's how I would feel if some stranger walked in on me naked.

Until then, I hadn't seen a lot of naked women's bodies. Even in college, when I lived with three women and shared a room with one of them, changing was always done in the bathroom. I might go to the gym with a friend, but we kept our backs to each other while changing into sports bras. It was the polite thing to do.

I suppose I learned these "manners" in my Catholic household, where talking about one's body was never encouraged, not that I even bothered. I was embarrassed to talk about my body, probably because I was always a little embarrassed of my body. It was never all that skinny or tight or shiny like the bodies I saw on the covers of magazines.

That might sound cliché, blaming magazines for poor body image, but when I didn't have anyone else to compare myself to, whom or what else could I blame?

Even with all the "rude" naked women in the locker room, we still signed up for a membership. And since then there's been a gradual change in my locker room attitude and decorum. In my early days, I would change in a bathroom stall. Eventually, I grew comfortable changing in the main area, but continued to turn my boobs towards the lockers when putting on my sports bra.

Now I whip all my clothes off without giving a damn who sees me.

They say that the best way to learn a language is to completely immerse yourself in it. Once I surrounded myself with naked female bodies, I actually started to understand that my body was nothing to be ashamed of. What I saw when I peeked sideways at ladies next to me or glanced in the mirror at ladies behind me is that the female body is practically the same on every woman. There are shoulders and breasts and tummies and thighs, and yes, they may vary in size, but I never find anyone's anything is better than the others'. In fact, I find them all equally beautiful. No body is shameful. They are all as they should be. And that made me realize, eventually, that maybe my body is beautiful, too.

I see little girls and teenagers walk through the locker room, and sometimes I wait to undress or cover up until they walk by, because I don't want to traumatize them or teach them something about the female body that perhaps their mother didn't want them to know. But they never seem shocked to be surrounded by flesh. They barely even notice. And I wonder what their body image is like, if they are more comfortable with themselves because they see so many normal women comfortable with themselves, comfortable enough to walk through a crowded room with no clothes on. When I cover up, aren't I just teaching them the shame and embarrassment I had to overcome?

Perhaps if I had been exposed to the female form more in my youth, it wouldn't have taken me so long to learn how to love my own body.

Now when I'm in the locker room and I see a clothed stranger getting a tour of the place, I let it all fly free. If she doesn't know the language here, I might as well immerse her in it on the first day.

RECLAIMING THE NARRATIVE

LESSONS FROM LIFE

by Heather Pease

Remember it is always darkest before the dawn
– Florence + The Machine

I have learned sometimes
I was my own abuser,
careening out of control
on a path of sabotage. Forgiveness
is meant for myself   first.
Healing has no concept of time.

I have learned not every fight
needs a battle; I was not made
for war. Death is not something
to wait for. Life is about connection,
education, is a journey of continual
growth.

I have learned, to stop looking back
at paths not taken.
To not drop my burdens, and lade
myself with others'.

I have learned, it is okay to ask for help,
let me say that again
It. Is. Okay. To. Ask. For. Help.
It is not okay to pretend. I am only fooling
myself.

I have learned being heard
doesn't mean I have to be loud,
but I will be loud for what I believe in!
Silence, like cancer, kills.
I have learned I am

comfortable with who I am,
most days. Not defined by anyone.
Labels are for clothing.

I have learned being funny doesn't
mean I have
to be the joke.
Only children have no
concept of regret.
Hugs have power; crying has it too.
The love I require is right in the mirror.

I have learned expression
is survival; I
bleed on paper to breathe.
Darkness is temporary, I now carry a pen
as a flashlight.

I have learned, I am an atheist.
It's okay if you're not.
I am a feminist. It is not okay
if you are not.
Integrity is everything.

I have learned
growth requires raw — real — truth.
I am a Survivor, that
means, I am strong.
I am fiercely loved. I trust in
that love completely.
My family is my universe,
my sun, moon, and stars.

I have learned words/ have
the power/ you give them.
To listen more than to speak.
To savor a moment, turn it intoa memory. Laughter should
never be held back.
I was born.
I have learned I am worthy
of this life.
I am worthy
of love.
I am worthy.

RED

by Nikki Marrone

Sometimes I leave the blood on my skin,
To remember that red is not the colour of violence.
And that I am not a victim waiting to happen.
This space between my legs is not a crime scene.
Red is not a blood stained sidewalk,
It is not the cut of a prostitute's[1] gown.
Sometimes I leave the blood on my skin,
For the ones who have no choice,
To remember those who wear it like war paint,
And to support those who wear it with shame.
This is no tear-stained apology,
Nor a problem to be solved.
This is a not something to be taken lightly,
Nor a burden heavily carried.
Sometimes I leave the blood on my skin,
To remind myself that being a woman,
Isn't something easily washed away.
To remind myself that being a woman,
Isn't unclean.

---

[1] The reference to a "prostitute's gown" is in reference to the media's negative portrayal of sex workers and how society still refers to women wearing red clothing or lipstick as 'slutty' or 'trying to draw attention to themselves.' When used in reference to women, the colour red is always negative or violent. The poem is a reclaiming of not only the colour but of our bodies, our sense of agency and identity. It is in no way intended as a slur toward, or a reflection of, the sex work industry.

LIVING DANGEROUSLY

by Emma Owens

She keeps keys between her fingers like Wolverine.
She lives on the third floor but checks the locks of her windows
obsessively.

She fears the night like a child might,
but now goblins are preferred company in the dark.

A friend, he's 5'10", asks for a movie night, but they go the park —
there are people there: mothers with kids who jump and run and play
and spin.

"What, you don't trust me? Why can't I come in?"
But no. She can't. Can't trust a 'him.'

When it comes to friendship or her life,
she decides she'd rather live.
She knows she can be more than just a wife —
that there's more the world can give.

She needs a new dresser. She asks her dad to contact the seller on
Messenger.

She does not retrieve it alone, even when a woman answers the phone.

The doorbell rings. She ordered pizza, but anxiety buzzes through her
brain like a fly.

She yells "I'll get it!" to the empty apartment
before she opens the door to some random guy.

At a party, she checks on her friends and they do the same.

All for one and one for all, it's almost a game.
No drinks left unattended.
God, I hope he's not offended
by rejection.

Precautions, she takes precautions.
She lives a normal life; how can that be brave?
She thrives in a society that would make her its slave.
She's a lightning bolt of indignation; she's the fourth-wave.

I am a Feminist and...

by Lex Elliott

I always knew that I was a feminist. What would confuse me sometimes were the additional clauses or explanations some people would
make following an admission of the same. I would always hear people
say crap like, "I don't consider myself a feminist because I don't hate
men," or "I'm kind of a feminist, but I am also for equality," or "I am a
feminist, but like not that kind of feminist." The associations made with
feminism are often skewed enough to make some of us roll our eyes.
I never really knew why until college, where I learned more about the
radical groups that were popularized during the second wave of feminism in the US. I learned about talk shows showcasing "men-hating
lesbians with an agenda" and the publication of books that labeled feminists as a "threat" to average American families. It became clear that,
without a closer look into what feminism actually meant, these popular
misconceptions became the misconstrued portrayal of feminism we can
still see today.

The class I have to thank for my deepened understanding of feminism
was taught by two very good professors. We covered the civil rights
movement, second wave feminism, and other impactful moments in
American history. Most of these lessons were packed with hot-but-
ton issues about gender, ethnicity, class, sexuality, and so many other
important issues. I was on board for everything we were doing in that
class, until it came time to receive feedback for our papers. I was given
all the standard things: lots of grammar corrections, suggestions for
clarity, and smiling faces next to the best parts of my paper! One com-
ment, though, stood out from the rest, and it remains one of the things
that helped solidify my identity as a feminist thinker.

My paper discussed the complexity and progressive examples of relationships in the work of the Beat Generation, while being careful not to
ignore the blatant sexism and misogyny the male writers had in their

work. I covered same-sex relationships, polyamory, and non-traditional heterosexual relationships, but one professor asked me to eliminate matters of bisexuality, specifically. I could not explain why this had bothered me so much, but it did. My young, petty self went into a defensive and immediately went to office hours to defend my claim. I was ready to go in on this professor until I stepped into the office and saw a huge banner behind the desk stating "FEMINISM." I was taken aback, and just listened to the critiques. The lesson didn't really click for me until years later...

Cut to me in the future, in graduate school where I was reading some article that discussed the popular use of "intersectionality" when talking about gender, sexuality, and race. In simple terms, this idea is not only about including representations and diversity in what we write, do, and think. It is about doing justice to the different identities that are present and being aware of the unique ways every identity complicates the concepts of gender, sexuality, race, class, and so many other things. And it clicked...maybe I should have done a better job of explaining why multiplicity in sexuality and relationships was so important in that one paper. Maybe through the lens of intersectionality, I could have better connected bisexuality and feminism. Maybe I just shouldn't have been so sensitive about the whole thing and understood how perspectives can differ and that can be an okay thing. Regardless, I am happy that I did not try and argue against the professor. We were both right, and all that was necessary was for me to better articulate the connection I always felt existed between feminism and all the identities that make us up.

To me, feminism always meant equality — an even playing field for everyone. Equality requires the coexistence of perspectives alongside each other despite their differences. While one professor was able to see the merit of what I had to say, the other focused on something different. Why could I not see that it was all just a matter of perspective? It would have saved me so much misplaced frustration. In the end, I learned that being able to understand difference is at the core of feminism. These differences do not take away from but, rather, add to feminism to make it more powerful. Equality cannot happen without empathy and understanding of the differences everyone brings based on who they are, where they are from, and what they've experienced.

As an queer person of color, sexuality and race have always been inseparably braided in my identification as a feminist. That's why I push to add more positive phrases to our admissions of being feminists. I have always tried to not take advantage of my privilege and perpetuate the social ideologies that exist against other genders. Instead, my goal is to use feminism as support for everyone who has been marginalized. If I want anything, it's to hear people using feminism as a means of connection and support, while using our differences to our advantage in making this movement even greater.

That's why I've adopted my own clauses to add:

"I am a feminist and support women of color."
"I am a feminist and support trans women."
"I am a feminist and support any individual experience."

THAT GUY

by Marc Cid

One high school morning
among the hallway haze
of *hey theres* and *what's ups*
and *geometry is bullshit,*
when are we gonna need
to know how to calculate
the area of an isosceles trapezoid
in real life, as the popular girls
exchanged hellos and hugs,
a guy from the in crowd walked up
to one in particular, his eyes measuring
the area of her curvature, and asked:
"Where's *my* hug?"
with slavering arms outstretched.

I hadn't happened upon the phrase *male entitlement*
yet. Wouldn't until college, until taking gender
studies and then complaining that *gender roles*
are bullshit, is this why my aunt never learned
how to refuel her car, why my uncle would refuse
to fill up the tank if he was angry with her,
is this why I learned how to calculate
the area of a grown man's tantrum
through my mother's rapidly rising pulse?

But watching that girl hesitate as she calculated
the consequences of choosing her own comfort
over the distended jaws of his anglerfish civility,
as the other schoolgirls made a wave
of microshrugs and forced laughs
at the jokes boys make, the jokes

with patriarchy as the setup
and femininity as the punchline,
I wrote my own formula for real life use:

to never demand a hug from a girl —
either directly or passive-aggressively —
so I wouldn't be my uncle,
so I wouldn't be my dad,
so I wouldn't be that guy.

Kicking Down the Walls of Physiology

by Sarah Krashefski

As a person, I genuinely thrive on the theme of extreme, and honestly enjoy the terror and excitement it can bring. There was a rainy day in high school where every outdoor sport was cancelled due to serious weather conditions, yet my coach instructed my soccer team and I to run five miles in the pouring rain. While running, I wasn't bothered by the feeling of constant wetness all over my body, because at that point we were so wet it felt like we were inside a swimming pool. On the other hand, I was fighting the constant urge to bail and sprint for shelter, because the rapid velocity of rain drops was tremendously painful on my face. They felt like sharp needles coming down from the sky. During our walk back to the locker rooms, all eyes were on us, especially the boys. With their mouths gaping open, eyes wide, these boys were in disbelief that the girls' soccer team trained in such harsh rain. Silently, my teammates and I walked completely drenched, creating puddles of water behind us, and exchanged our own looks of disbelief with each other. The only difference was that my teammates' expressions and my own identified the realization that every male sports team lounged under dry shelter, while we were under attack by shooting rain drops. We as young women accomplished something much more gratifying than physical achievement that day in the rain.

My passion was soccer from a very young age. The drive I felt for soccer eventually aided my recruitment into club travel soccer leagues at eleven years old. I was pushed to my limits by my club coaches, who used to play professional soccer. I learned early on that there will always be someone better, but the defining attribute of every player may be unique and varied from each individual. By exerting myself, I honed in on my special skills. I was perhaps the third fastest runner, but not the fastest. I was perhaps the second-best defender, but not the best. Internally, I would tell myself *there*

135

will always be someone who is physically more equipped for the game, but mentally you are your own captain. My natural abilities to never give up, always fight until I am the winner, envision the play before it would happen, and make a significant difference on the field was my uniqueness. Finding my significant ability in soccer enticed me to be the best I could be at it. I did this not to outshine other players, but for my own self-gratification. At the end of the day, my internal validation was what mattered, not my parents, not my coach, and definitely not my peers.

Unfortunately, the internal voice for others can be less inspiring and more so detrimental to overcoming gender inequality. I grew up with an older brother who viewed me as much as a competitor as his peers, because he understood my unique skills as a person and didn't underestimate my smaller frame. I was raised by a tomboy mother who never told me "no" when I would ask to play tackle football with the boys for fun. I was encouraged by my father, who nurtured my athletic and intellectual abilities. He didn't assume I liked pink—because I didn't, and he definitely didn't perceive my brother's athletic ability and intellect as superior to mine. Therefore, I was raised to shoot for the stars and not let others tell me "no" when it came to my ability to achieve what I want in life.

Daily, I see women I care about, and female strangers who are taken advantage of due to their gender. Women need to stand up for other women; men need to stand up for women; and women need to stand up for men in return. Therefore, people just need to stand up for what is right and essentially each other when in time of need.

On my first day of university co-ed soccer I only counted three other female soccer players in the league. We were quickly separated based on the color of our shirts, and women were methodically divided onto one team each.

The whistle blew, and off we were. I was the only woman on my team, and immediately my teammates didn't trust me. Each one of them hesitated to pass me the ball, even if I was open and calling for it. This form of teamwork left me with one choice—steal the ball from the other team. So, that's what I did. I fought tooth and nail for the ball, whenever it came near and proved myself by passing it to the same teammates that avoided me before; showing that I was one of them. Once we started to play more like a team, they understood exactly what my brother did—I was the biggest threat on the field. I utilized my momentum and smaller frame to body check every single player who wasn't on my team. Whenever I had the ball, I refused to let the other team possess it. And to top it off, I created amazing plays on the goal by always anticipating one step ahead. Towards the end of the first half, the other team was triple guarding me.

I got to know a few of the men on my team, and enjoyed them as teammates and playing with them on a weekly basis, but there was one man I did not. His name was Jeff.

"Hey Sarah, nice playing out there, I couldn't believe it!" Jeff gestured enthusiastically.

"Ah thanks, but what do you mean?" I looked at him puzzled.

"Well, you know, for a girl."

He walked past me and smugly patted me on the back, like a dog who did a new trick.

This was the start of a very difficult season, where I was constantly picking my battles on when to address sexist comments by competitors and my own team, because frankly they happened so damn often.

Before one of our games, our team was gossiping in a circle near me. As I peeled off one of my ear buds, I heard Jeff's annoying voice.

"Oh my gosh, we're going to murder this team. They have like four girls." A few of the guys laughed along with Jeff as the others stood there silent. Quickly, I walked up to Jeff.

"Jeff, seriously?" I questioned him.

"What's up Sarah?"

"Why are you insinuating that the opposing team will lose because they have more women?"

"What do you mean? I'm not insinuating anything… It's a fact." Jeff looked at me with a confused expression.

"I want you to know that everything you just said and many comments in the past can be perceived as sexist and degrading towards women." My eyes locked onto his for a few seconds, before he looked away.

"Woah there… That's not what I meant at all."

"Then, what did you mean Jeff?" I sighed while leaning my hand on my hip.

"I'm simply saying that men are better than women. It's proven by physiology that we are built stronger and have more physical ability, especially in sports." Now, the whole team was surrounding us and yet, are silent.

"So, are you saying you're a better soccer player than me?"

"No, Sarah, no. That is not what I'm saying. You're different than most girls. You're the exception. You're way better than me and practically the best player on the team. I'm sorry if my comments offended you, but that was not my intention. I wasn't talking about you." Jeff backed off from me to seem less threatening.

"See Jeff, that's where you're wrong. I'm not the exception. I'm a regular woman just like the ones right over there." I point vigorously with anger.

"I'm good at soccer not because I have an abnormal natural ability that goes against your physiology theory. I simply just worked hard. I worked my whole life to be where I am and to counteract any disadvantages I may have. I am definitely not faster than you, nor stronger than you, yet I am still a better soccer player than most of the men here. Therefore, your comments are sexist no matter how you intended them." At this point, I was trying so hard not to punch Jeff's misogynistic hole he thinks is a mouth.

"Okay Sarah, okay. Can we just agree to disagree?" He shrugged his shoulders and retreated to the restroom. As I looked around, the rest of my teammates dispersed, except one man who was sitting on the benches.

"What do you think? Do you agree with him?" I turned to the tall man with black braids that hovered over his shoulders.

"No." He said simply, but firmly.

I tilted my head for a second, confused.

"Wait... if you didn't agree with him then why didn't you say anything?"

"I didn't want to get involved with the drama, to be honest."

138

PHOENIX

by Nikki Marrone

I was told to wait,
For a man to come my way.
The one who would wear the crown,
And ride the golden mare.
Whose stare would have me enamoured for a lifetime,
A man so great I would prostrate myself on an altar of "love."
Devote myself to deities of death and destruction.
Find joy in the cleansing fire of chaos
and crumbling brick of derelict foundations.
They never stopped to warn me of false prophets.
Those who never learnt the difference between taking and giving.
Who think no means convince me.
Who take your reluctance for lack of conviction.
They soothe salt-licked wounds at the fire inside of you.
Abuse the privilege of your kindness,
While you learn the mantras of their madness.
Map scar to scar,
Until their songs of sadness,
Become the lullabies that soothe your own neurosis.
You will try to tame them.
Be the eye in the centre of the storm,
Or the milk in their veins.
But you are no antidote
No cleansing liquid
You are nothing but matter but what matters most is you.

So do not worship at the feet of those that kick you down,
Stand upon your ankles and wait for you to stand.
Do not seek comfort from the hands that hurt you.
That stained you black and blue.
Instead rise from the ashes of your grave

To be reborn,
Like leaves burnt bare for the fallen.
Striped back like the bones in shattered rib cages,
Air torn straight from the lungs,
Drowning on dry land.
Because you are not weak for needing trigger warnings.
Not damaged.
Not broken.
Not used.
Not a victim.

You do not stay for the ones who love you,
If you no longer love yourself.

LITTLE ONE

by S.Dennison

Little One,

You will be "should" on in a thousand ways before you understand what it means to be a woman. You will "should" on yourself a hundred-thousand more. You will be shown in ten-thousand ways that the body you inhabit is wrong.

The assembly will rule that you are less important than the load they couldn't account for or that scholarship they could.

You will push these things out of your mind deep into the pockets of the baggy jeans you wear when you're out after dark with your friends in Portland or Denver or Anchorage that time the cabby told you to carry the bear mace in your hand on your way back to your AirBnB after class because, "Girls like you, go missing around there."

You will wear red flannel and your brother's black beanie to cover your curls.

Later, you will hide your body in black button-downs and burgundy blazers as you pace the front of your classroom while you lecture. You will weave the keys of the house you own, the car you bought, and the office where you're tenured in-between the fingers of your fist. It's a habit you picked up back when you learned to push these things out of your mind deep into the pockets of your trousers as you did those long walks home when you passed by all those Brocks, or Bretts, or Dons, or whoever.

But what's in a name when they all sound the same? Don't fall for that either.

What it means to be a woman is to pull out the pieces of everything that's broken and hold them in your hands. Sort what is yours to carry and what isn't. It will be hard to know the difference.

All you must do, for now, is look. There is more to do later.

Those who haven't seen will call you names. Some will call you nasty. The polite ones will call you woke. Take these as compliments and stick them in your pocket with all the other broken bits. This is your confetti. Throw it when you understand.

It is not revolutionary to see yourself as whole. Many have profited from thinking you're broken. It is not revolutionary to see yourself as whole.

Teach this to yourself and others. No one can show you how — only reasons that you must. Take what you need from this one —

My mother and grandmother never left the house without painting rouge on their cheeks.

After my mother lost her hair, she put on a wig. In the second year of radiation, she switched to fleece hats.

My grandmother was a dressmaker who lived through the Dust Bowl. Buried a husband and daughter, then memory.

She and my mother raised me, together with a beast. That C-letter word — Cancer. You may be called a different one.

The first time I understood what it meant to be a woman was when my mother, dying of cancer, bundled up in a blanket with a chemo pouch in a fanny pack.

A tube wound its way up her swollen abdomen into the permanent port installed above her heart. She sat out outside in the cold spring of the Colorado foothills in a lawn chair, mid-chemo session, just to watch me play in a soccer game.

I learned what it meant to be a woman when I saw my grandmother cry.

I learned what it meant to be a woman when my mother said in the hospice lobby, that she hoped we had come to terms with her dying, and when I ran as fast as I could out of the double-doors into the courtyard.

I learned that there is pain when a girl becomes a woman and that sometimes it hurts so bad that you fall to your knees in front of statues you aren't even sure you believe in.

I learned what it meant to be a woman when I sang at her funeral when I was eleven.

I learned what it meant to be a good woman when I saw that there weren't enough seats to house the people who loved her.

My life, so far, has been filled with trying to sort what it means to be a good woman and I think, for now, it is that line somewhere between strength and grace.

After my mother passed, someone else stepped in. That someone passed this April from a disease that tried to take her voice but couldn't.

You, too, will fight a disease that will try to take your voice. It will sometimes. And when it does, remember your strength and grace.

We all will lose our mothers so we must become for each other what they were or we wished they were for us.

It is not revolutionary to see yourself as whole. Teach this to yourself and others.

ON TAKING ADVICE

by Nadia F. Alamah

they will tell you so many things,
and most of them will not prove to be true.
they will say that one's too far away, go someplace closer,
and surely you will drown.
you'll hear a lot of no and be expected, when asked, to say yes.
when they give you advice it will be with a vision in mind.
she will marry a man whose face is like hers,
one she has to listen to, one that won't care how pretty she is
as long as she is modest and lives by his standards,
she will have his children and if she wants a job it will be to keep her busy,
it should be something easy that won't take away from her house and kids
they give me advice thinking I will become like my community
and they see my wild side as an accessory of youth, not something of being,
of desperate yearning for escape and truth, they say don't climb too high
because the fall will break your bones and still their kids throw
stones every day
and I wait, and wonder why everyone will say something to you,
everyone thinks their words are gold bricks and they enjoy the glint
of metal
and their reflections in the bar and the sour taste of wanting
and they will expect you to take less and say thank you and please don't
and yes, always yes and never no, they will expect you to listen
and nod your head and agree, and many of them will never stop themselves
to listen to you and hear what you want,
and if then it will be with a bandage,
or a prescription, or a remedy for your life and thinking, and this is
why I left,
because the words caught in my net were not the kind I liked to keep,
and they swirled and muddied the waters until I couldn't see the sun's light
refracted when I was doing my best to catch the moon,
by searching for the truths in her face mirrored below,

I am doing the groundwork
and looking inward and that is how I know,
that somewhere out there are the answers and I will find them
through grit and resolve, I am searching for kindness
in the moonfaces of my aunts and mother and grandmother
and that is how I sift the truths, their advice may not take me
the route that I dream of but in the shadows lie some promise,
that no matter which current I surf the destination will be somewhere
just over the horizon, and I need to paddle and keep swimming
and grit my teeth and bear the burden for just another day,
that despite how the critics bite my arms and neck and back
as I beat back their merciless sounds on the wind and sweat away the sun,
I will hold fast and lift my sails and keep my head held high and carry on,
there are those out there who will get and really see me,
who will not try to restrain me with ropes, or pack my heart into a box,
expecting it to be as pristine as the day I left it, and I say to you
never disconnect yourself to satisfy the passing whims of others,
be brave and bold and as unconventional as you dare to stretch and see
that when they say you'll fall, it's because you've let them clip your wings,
and because you haven't, you'll soar, and savor the limitlessness of being.

You 2.0

by Helen Rosenau, Your Jewish Fairy Godmother

Most of us spend too much time worried about how others see us, judge us, or even overlook us completely. We fret about seeing our deepest secrets reflected in their eyes. Too often we forget: we get to choose who/how we want to be in the world. We have that authority 100%. And fuckit to those who don't love and appreciate us.

Ok, I'm lying a little. On a bad hair day, or after a horrible date, you'd have to be Buddha or Jesus not to feel a tad skittish. But that's trivial compared to figuring out the deep stuff, like Who am I? Or what your core is made of and how it hangs together. And then, yikes, there's how you go into the world and how you respond to praise and/or rejection.

Teenager = What's Been You 1.0 is morphing into a new you, *You 2.0.* Here's the fabulous and terrifying news: you get to write her owner's manual, her script.

Maybe you've already excelled at something. Good on you. But most teens have been their parents' child, classmate's buddy, and a slightly-taken-for-granted member of various groups. As you emerge from being "a kid," you gain new status. Countless cultures honor that shift with ceremonies and rituals. Some are great parties; others more painful.

In *The Messy Joys of Being Human* there's a chapter called "Stripes and Plaids" about two baby dahlias, both labeled Orange Ball, which neither became. Instead they're mis-matched sisters: one soft pink/white, the other spiky yellow/red. Hard on the eyes; so I added two plucked from a neighbor's free pile. One became an orange ball, the other fiery, ruby red, with an unopened bloom in its center.

That's teenager-dom: all your incredible potential, fiercely contained in a tight bud. Its true nature hidden, revealing in peeks and spurts.

You know how it is. You find a new band or food and obsess, texting and telling everyone how fab it is. You pick a color for a day or week, just to play with how you feel in it. Ditto every impulse from morning till bed. You're playing in the jeans store of life. Having fun and laughing at the mirror, in a loving kind of way.

You Now, You 2.0, and all the next Yous are the best binge-watch ever. Each one emerges, has adventures, sparkles and spins, and then, sometimes in a quick blip and sometimes after a tough slow slog, you change again. They're a busy bunch but so mesmerizing. You'll adore some of these future selves and reject (or try to) other mini-incarnations. Eventually you'll thank them all, even if they were tough teachers in their prime.

Just being teenaged-you takes amazing amounts of time and attention. So much that you might forget you're supposed to be the You whom you've been, the one that other folks are expecting to relate to. As 2.0 gets stronger, she'll start showing up more often, even without you planning, some bold version of the went-to-school-naked dream. She does things former You didn't. You'll raise your hand more (or less) often, make new friends, decide you want to be part of a different pod of folks. You might speak your truth out loud (oops!) to your opinionated (idiot) uncle because he was too loud to keep blocking out. In time, you'll learn how to wield your new super powers, plus also get fab new skills to command attention and support when you want and need it. But for now it's all brewing up a storm you can't always control. You'll blow it often. We all do.

You walk around knowing there's A Dramatic Reveal primping and pacing. You know she's not quite ripe. But you don't wanna blink and miss the big splash. First you want to (sorta have to) figure out this new you. Get to know her a whole lot better. Treat her like your new best friend. Pizza and planning, whispering and laughing into the wee hours about how you'll burst open into fabulous splendor.

Things are changing, inside and out. Your body has new surprises and delights. Your mind is moving faster than the speed of light. Some days it can feel like there's just too much happening. Even if no one else can see, inside the You they know and expect, something magical is brewing.

Remember, writing your 2.0 script isn't a one-time homework assignment you should rush to finish. The *Who Am I?* story lasts a lifetime, and this is your first big chance to write the rules.

You'll want to feel secure wearing 2.0 before more than some test drives. You'll wanna see what she's capable of, like those fabulous early scenes in *Wonder Woman*, where she's training and sparring, before you embrace your 2.0.

Don't bother. Waiting until you grok this next You can be the most anti-feminist thing you will ever do. Like not letting other people's expectations or judgments define you, why limit yourself to a finite idea of self? You're going to change and evolve and grow as long as you're alive. Hooray! That next You will continue to shift and refine. I hope you transform until the end of your days. Up ahead are You 3.0, 4.0, and more. Enjoy each and every one of them. Revel in their victories and learn from their disasters. Not only is life not a straight line, but the curves and spins can be the best, and certainly the most exciting, times, assuming you survive them in good health and freedom.

The good news and the bad: no matter which You that you decide to play in or wrestle with, it's only for a while. Whoever you become after that will be in charge next. She'll write the rules, and choose the loves and adventures. So love this now You completely. Give her hope and encouragement and the power to resist judgment, from herself and others. Tell her what you most want, and help her to make it so.

I hope 2.0 is a good guide for you. Ask her regularly what comes next. Then listen, really really listen. She will send you signs and portents in sweet and mysterious ways. Being in the now will help you notice what they're telling you. Give 2.0 mostly what she wants (without landing in horrible trouble or jail). Try to feel where she is leading you. Keep reminding yourself, you get to choose.

Create a 2.0 that makes you feel most whole. As in, being the next You shouldn't take a fuckload of work to sustain. Be a 2.0 who wakes up happy, sharp, confident. Ready to navigate yesterday's legacy and big life goals. Have her back, as she's got yours.

On a good day, go into the world to love, laugh, and do battle. Be curious and fabulous, in all your smart and charming ways. Be brave, generous, and kind. Do good for yourself and for others. On a bad day, stay closer to your safe people and places. Then go home to pace, grumble, and wail. Thrash around until you know where the bad vibes came from. Maybe some mood is working you like a bad zit. Or a crappy thing someone said or did that you just can't flush. Get clear on how you'd like the world to be and feel instead.

Safety Tip: On a Very Very Very Bad Day, avoid being impetuous. Trust me, the cleanup just isn't worth it. Eat chocolate, chips, or both. Rock it out. Call your bestie. Do NOT send or post anything.

The world is filled with rules and people who want you to obey them. Some keep society from collapsing, but can seem arbitrary and detestable. What made sense until now can seem oh so confining.

But you're not eighteen. Tick-tock. Tick-tock. Play the long game. Every day you're a smidgen closer. Then you can screw up when- and how- ever you like. (Though honestly, no matter your age, choose your battles. Life will shove enough crap in your path to keep you busy and engaged without looking for trouble.)

Values matter. A lot. Know what you believe, what you stand for, what you're willing to put up with, and where your boundaries are. Know you deserve respect, just for being you. Don't be pushed around by anyone trying to move you where you don't want to go. You get the last vote in everything: from what you eat, to whom you love, or where and how you pray. Every morning remind yourself you are strong and independent; watch out for anyone who tries to change that.

The universe is full of clues to help make this time easier. Pay close attention to whatever your inner voice is telling you, even if it sounds like static. Look for hints about which way to go. They often show up as "coincidences" (aka synchronicities). Take good notes. The sooner you notice whatever's unfolding, the easier the message will land.

Your 2.0 script is yours to make real. You can't make it happen on your own or just by wanting it. If wanting was enough we'd all be in different versions of us. Balancing acceptance and desire is effing tricky. It's the ultimate highwire act of being human. Setting goals and intentions ups the odds of getting closer to where you want to go. Plus, if you get lost, you can wander looking for a door to your destination. Warning: not much is as you imagine it will be. And the journey has good surprises as well as scary ones.

One way or another, there's important self-knowing up ahead. I hope you run happily to greet 2.0, 3.0, 4.0 and the more who're coming.

Like yourself when you look in the mirror. Enjoy who's smiling back. Fuck the flaws. You're already fabulous, and there is so much more splendor to come. Your body will be different in a month, a year, a decade, and be-

150

yond. It will give you happiness beyond measure, and surprises you will love and hate. Drop the judgments as soon as you can. Play with your style till you get it right, whether that takes a day or a decade.

Do something stretchy like yoga that'll keep your joints in tune. You'll feel lighter in your body and soul. Plus your older self will send you showers of gratitude.

Figure out your own beliefs and values. Don't swallow someone else's (be that a parent, teacher, or pal) without questioning. Not one answer fits every person, place, or time. Explore the imagery and metaphors of many spiritual, artistic, and culinary paths. There are fundamental truths in each of them, whether you embrace it or not.

Keep your taste buds for life ready, curious, and open. Become a reader. Toss out keywords of things you care about or wish you did. (Find me if you want ideas.) Wander in many different cultures, geographies, and timelines. Learn to say *Hello* in a couple of languages.

Have fabulous friends. Wonderful, smart, comfy, energetically bright friends. People who make you laugh and let you cry. People who've got your back on the worst day and with whom you celebrate on your best. People you can talk to about whatever you want. Who know what you mean when you tell a story. Who ask the right questions and call you on your crap, in a way you will listen to, especially when you most need them to.

Dating, and even friendship, can get complicated. Big Tip: Them wanting you is not enough; you have to want them back. Bad News: It takes a while to figure this part of life out. Where to set the bar: someone who adores your best parts and tolerates your worst with patience and humor. Folks who didn't have taught me lots, and I hated every second of while it was happening.

"Choose wisely" is the ultimate mantra. Its dark side will also teach you, but there's heartache and bruising when you blow it. Your heart will love and break, ache and heal, so many times more than you can possibly imagine. Avoid getting so lost in someone that you let them re-write your script. You Now, You 2.0, You Next, and You After That should always get the last vote.

Have safety zones: people you can tell your worst and scariest. If they're not the ones they're supposed to be (like your family), find folks you trust. If bullying or abuse happens, speak up until you find someone with the power to make it stop. Bad shit isn't your fault, but you do have a responsibility to act.

Avoid shame, guilt, and emotional toxicity as best you can. Don't stuff bad feelings in, even if it's so much easier in the moment. You won't like the side effects, let alone the nasty crap their gremlins will pull, usually when you least expect or can cope. None of us gets out without hurting. Learn how to take good care of yourself in ways that don't sabotage your big hopes.

Be someone people care about. Who they want to talk to about what really matters to them. Be generous and kind, and call those people towards you. Love them every day; tell them often. Life can be scary. Friends matter.

Take regular chunks of down time. Go for walks or dance, make music or art. Be with just you on a regular basis, and yes that means no screens for an hour (okay, twenty minutes before you peek).

Meditate. Just do it. I don't care if it's sitting, walking, or staring, in a sanctuary, nature, or even your room. But at least five minutes a day give yourself absolute quiet time. Zero responsibilities. Just saying, *I'm going to meditate* should get you respectful compliance (even from adults). And the benefits are too many to count.

Don't be pet-less for too long: cat, dog, or whatever critters you adore. Let their unconditional love open your heart.

Have fabulous romances and great sex. Don't worry about your kinks or curiosities because everybody has some. Treat your partners and lovers with the care you want from them. Play, explore, and enjoy, hopefully with people who are worthy of your trust.

Learn to ask for forgiveness. Just like you're gonna get your heart bruised, it's inevitable that you'll hurt other people, intentionally or not. Forgive others with grace as a pay it forward; you'll be the one needing it some day.

Hone your psychic skills. Practice feeling the subtle currents of a room. See how energy sparkles and sparks. Learn to trust your gut. Though sadly I promise that you'll make some monumental errors of judgment. They will cost you tears and time. That's part of how you'll learn.

152

Here's the secret. The one people call The Law of Attraction. Sadly it's not as simple as *Gimme*.... You are guaranteed infinite access and ongoing communication with what I call "the world of the unseen," the energies that animate creation. That conversation matters, however you call it, practice, and make ritual or play with it.

I hope you learn to enjoy what comes, though it's rarely in the ways you will imagine or ask for it. Don't get me wrong. It's not about settling for less, but about timing and doing your karmic homework. As 2.0 becomes 3.0 and beyond, she'll even begin to savor the really hard core work of *Who am I and what am I here to do in this world?*. I hope you can make that soul searching a game.

Desires that come from goodness tend to get to the front of the karma line. The "I want this now, dammit, so gimme!" wants not so much. Which is why I say the inner stuff (generosity, gratitude, and your strength of self) is a good starting point for most of life. Be a person who's here to do good as well as to receive it. Then the path you'll travel will be softer and easier, with fewer chasms or demons lurking, real or metaphorical.

Vote. As soon as you can and every time. It matters. Speak your truth, whatever it becomes, and try to heal this broken world.

Try and avoid the terrible habits and cultivate the ones that make you feel spiffy and sharp. You'll want a healthy brain and body down the road, so treat them as well as you can. Moderation isn't always fun, but notice when you arc out too far for too long.

Life is unpredictable and non-linear beyond human comprehension. Give thanks when things happen mostly the way you want. I hope the tough times end quickly, and that you find your way through and past them. Breathe deeply either way. Know that you'll make incredibly stupid mistakes in good times and in bad. But don't define yourself by them. Keep visioning the next best you and aspire to become her.

Learn to bounce. You'll get so many chances between this you and the last. Resilience and laughter can make or break each day. I pray you even wake up laughing in your dreams.

Remember those budding dahlias, the ones that opened last? When their time comes, they do it in the most incredible splendor. They get more and more beautiful with each slow reveal. And watching always makes you feel like there's so much more beauty to come. That's your future, and your now.

LETTERS FROM THE EDITORS

As with any creative project, we all came into the making of this book with our own hopes and expectations of what we were making. Being a single mom to a very strong-willed boy, it was important to me from the very beginning to create a book about feminism that would be useful in having conversations with young men as well as women. I wanted a book that would help young people understand they were seen and had a place to be heard as well. I wanted to give them hope for the future. But as I began reading the submissions for this collection, I was the one who was overwhelmed by a feeling of hope for the first time in years—hope for our future generations of feminists, and faith that they will come from all walks of life. Intersectional feminism has been important to our press from the very beginning, and with the events of 2020 unfolding in the middle of trying to create this book, these stories became more important than ever.

I hope that this book leaves you with the same sense of hope and pride that I feel every time I read these stories. I hope that it helps you have conversations about women's rights so we can carry on the torch for Ruth Bader Ginsburg. I hope that it helps young men understand their role in the fight for equality. I hope that it helps young women lift up their voices and rejoice in their bodies and their spirit alike. But most of all, I hope the words of these amazing writers help readers to feel connected in a time when we need it most.

Much Love and Respect,
Stephanie

Putting this book together was nothing like I expected it to be. When we put out a call for anecdotes, essays, and poems about feminism and growing up, I had no idea we would get such a variety of voices and stories. Some of our contributors tackled worldwide issues, and some of them shared their deeply personal experiences. I think the wide breadth of topics and approaches represented here really speaks to both the process of growing up and the process of coming to understand and define feminism and gender equality. No two people have the same experiences, but we can still connect with and support each other while we figure it all out.

This is not the definitive guide to anything. Rather, I hope that this book and the amazing authors in it give you the chance to feel seen, learn something new, and engage in the conversation. We're all learning, growing, and doing the best we can to build the world we want to live in. Thanks for being part of this journey, dear reader. I hope to see you in our next book!

Best,
Christina

Growing up, people always told me I fell into the "one of the guys" trope. Maybe it started because my kindergarten class only had 4 girls including me. Or because my dad was the dominant voice and role model in our home, until I grew and realized what a resilient person my mother was. Or in highschool when I wanted to spend all my time with the jocks because 'they're funny' and 'less drama' than girls.

It wasn't until college that I began to understand the gender dynamics that had been in-play my whole life. I wasn't "one of the guys." I was reaching to be equal to them. And with the help of some beautiful female friends, it was time to level the playing field.

It felt so refreshing to read the submissions to this collection for the first time. And time and time again. They make me laugh, cry, reflect... I relate to so many of these authors and am so proud of the ones who shared the hard to talk about things. More than anything this guide is about supporting our fellow ladies, whether we know their exact struggle or not. You don't need to be "one of the guys" because you deserve so much better as yourself, and as a woman.

Rage on,
Megan

Author Biographies

Nadia F. Alamah

Nadia F. Alamah is a Lebanese American writer, poet, and visual artist who moved to Southern California from Flint, Michigan a few years ago, and who now has three places she calls home. Alamah recently published her illustrated chapbook of poems, Yalla Habibi: poems in 3arabeezi, where she begins to explore her Lebanese American identity via her poetry (previously it's all been abstract, love, scifi/fantasy and nature). She has otherwise focused on creation of community-centric arts projects and workshops in Flint prior to relocating to the West Coast.

Sana Asifriyaz

Sana Asifriyaz is a high school student at Rolling Hills Preparatory School, passionately studying subjects from humanities to various sciences. She actively participates in several school clubs, including Feminist Union, in which she and other schoolmates create a safe platform to discuss relevant topics and share their opinions, and leads Cakes for Causes, in which she helps raise funds to donate to local charities. She loves learning about new perspectives and other phenomena as she advocates for universal education.

Many of her written works remain currently unpublished, and they range from poetry and vignettes, critical essays, to graphic novellas and other short stories. Her purpose is to amplify her voice and others' through her visual and literary art. She works toward exploring and creating new projects and publishing previous works.

She lives in Los Angeles, California, with her parents, sister, and grandma. Her free time activities (besides writing) include watching and critically analyzing books and movies, walking, traveling around the world, and playing cards with her family.

Ra Avis

Ra Avis is the author of Sack Nasty: Prison Poetry (2016), Dinosaur-Hearted (2018), and Flowers and Stars (2018). She is a once-upon-a-time inmate, a reluctantly-optimistic widow, and a generational storyteller. Ra reads her poetry live at events throughout Southern California, and writes regularly at Rarasaur.com.

Kate Autumn Bokoles

I am autistic, disabled, queer and an advocate for neurodiversity and inclusivity in the widest and deepest possible definitions of the word. I love words as art, but I do not think in words, and I believe that words can only go so far to bring balance and equality back into the ecosystem that we live within. I am fascinated by permaculture design and I am coming to believe that the interdependency of nature may be the only true model for the justice and equality that we seek.

Julia Cheng

Julia Cheng is a writer based in the San Francisco Bay Area. She received her BA in English from CSU Channel Islands and writes about her interests such as personal finance, yoga, intersectional feminism, or anything else. Julia spends her free time contemplating her purpose in life as well as playing board games.

Marc Cid

Marc Cid is a Filipino-American poet who performs regularly in Long Beach, Orange, and other parts of Southern California. His upcoming book, Your Funeral Sucked, By The Way, a book of poetry concerning suicide ideation, bereavement, and stigmatization, will be published by Silver Star Laboratory at the end of the year.

S. Dennison

I was born and raised in the Colorado foothills. Then, after my first real brush with life, was transplanted to an extinct-gold-rush-town-turned-Atlantic City and finished up my tweens in a mountain town called Central City. More life. More transplants. So, I headed east and north to the Great Lakes and finished off what was left of childhood on the shores of Lake Michigan on the very tip of the Door County Peninsula. College took me to Bemidji, Minnesota. There, I completed a Bachelor's of Fine Arts in Creative and Professional Writing then a Master's in English focusing on Composition/Rhetoric. During this time, I piece-mealed a life working as an adjunct and youth-crisis counselor. Winters were hard and life got to be that way too, so I packed up and followed the OR trail west and accepted a position as faculty at a community college here in Oregon that has afforded me with a writing desk and a little space to carve out the beginnings of a writerly life. This last sum-mer, I returned to school to pursue a Master of Fine Arts in the Univer-sity of Alaska Anchorage's low-residency program.

Amon Elise

Amon Elise is the intersection of a writer, a yogi and a sensualist. Her vision of poetry as the ultimate medium of expression forces her audi-ence to ask questions and examine themselves. Originally from Florida, she now resides in Los Angeles and is making a name for herself in their active poetry community. Catch her on any given night at an open mic speaking truth. May her words move you.

Alexander Elliott

Alexander has been an avid admirer of stories in all their forms since he was a kid. After his studies in sunny San Diego, California, he relocated to the snowy wonderland of New England to explore what life has to offer.

Queen Ex

Queen Ex is a Los Angeles-born poet who started writing at age 12 and performing spoken word at age 16 in Oakland. Three years later, her writing became works of fiction that remained unpublished as she pursued a communications career in her hometown. As a poet she toured the L.A. indie scene, won a Rising Star Music Award in 2014, was briefly an erotic fiction ghostwriter, and worked with various entertainment professionals while studying media communications at Full Sail University. In 2015, her work as a host and production assistant on Callywood Media Network founded her ambitions to produce more podcasts and eventually ra-dio-plays. Two years later, she joined the Community Literature Initiative Program and became the author she dreamed she could be. In 2019, her first collection of fiction, HIDDEN MOMENTS, was published by World Stage Press. Periodically she gives guest lectures on the creative process, writes for online publications, and recites poetry at events. She currently lives in Los Angeles and expects to publish more works in the future.

Linda Ferguson

Linda Ferguson has won awards for her poetry and lyrical nonfiction and been nominated for a Pushcart Prize for both fiction and poetry. Her poetry chapbook, Baila Conmigo, was published by Dancing Girl Press. As a writing teacher, she has a passion for helping students explore new territory. https://bylindaferguson.blogspot.com/.

Jennifer Furner

Jennifer Furner has her Master's in Literature, and she lives in Grand Rapids with her husband and daughter. She is a freelance writer and editor, a library employee, and is currently working on publishing her first memoir. She has a forthcoming essay that will be published in Akashic Book's column 'Terrible Twosdays.'

Samyukta Iyer

Samyukta Iyer is a 16 year old STEAM-inist who uses and combines her passions for writing, music, science, and leadership to change the world and solve issues through empowerment and education. Her work has won awards such as the Poetry Society's Foyle Young Poet of the Year Awards, L.Ron Hubbard Science Fiction Contest, Ringling College of Art and Design Creative Writing Contest, National PTA Reflections Contest, and many more. She writes to inform, explain, and explore her world and the worlds of others.

Karisma Jaini

My name is Karisma Jaini. I am 16 and currently a junior in high school. I've been writing for as long as I can recall, but I started writing more seriously this past year. I wanted to pay homage to the women who have taught me everything I know. I love them more than anything else.

Hannah Jeoung

My human title is Hannah Jeoung, and I am a 17-year-old high school senior at Granada Hills Charter High School. Writing stories and poems has always been a personally important hobby that helped me express what I couldn't in spoken words. Since I have often found it hard to talk about feminism with those around me - especially since the Korean culture I grew up with is very patriarchal and my friends are mostly guys - I am grateful for this opportunity to have a voice in such an important issue.

Amanda Jess

Amanda Jess is a Nova Scotia-based journalist and writer who has covered the courts, municipal politics, arts and business. She recently graduated from the University of King's College with a Master of Fine Arts in Creative Nonfiction. She specializes in gender and LGBTQ+ issues, and proudly owns the label feminist.

Israa Kawsar

My name is Israa Kawsar and I am 17 years old. This is a message to everyone in the world because we need a daily reminder to appreciate what we have.

Yousra Kawsar

My name is Yousra Kawsar, I'm 16 years old and this is for everyone out there who feels suffocated by the world.

Sarah Krashefski

After Sarah Krashefski graduated from Ventura College as an Associate of Science in Engineering, she switched her major to pursue her dream of studying Creative Writing. With a Bachelor's of Arts degree in English and an Emphasis in Creative Writing from California State University Channel Islands, Sarah utilized her joint specializations of science and english as a Technical Editor to enter the aerospace sector of technology and engineering. While in college Sarah founded an academic non-profit organization called "The English Club" where she developed a community of Readers, Writers, and Educators. Sarah enjoys not only writing creative non-fiction, but also short story fiction and poetry. In Sarah's downtime she enjoys the outdoors, reading, coaching soccer, and rock climbing.

Eve Lyons

My name is Eve Lyons. I am a poet and fiction writer living in the Boston area. My work has appeared in Lilith. Hip Mama, Mutha Magazine, Word Riot, Dead Mule of Southern Literature, as well as other magazines and several anthologies. My first book of poetry is due out in May of 2020 by WordTech Communications.

Nikki Marrone

Nikki Marrone is a published poet, photographer, artist and mother. When she's not wandering around the world documenting her adventures, she splits her time between performing, running events and workshop leading. She is the winner of multiple Poetry Slams and has featured at various spoken word nights and festivals around the world.

Aisha Hussain

Aisha Husain is a Pakistani-English American poet and creative writer. Her work explores the body, culture and traditions, tensions and silences, and the politics and formation of identity. Husain received her BFA from Chapman University and is currently working on her MA in American Studies from California State University Fullerton.

Sophia Moore

Sophia Moore is a teen writer, based in California. She is fairly new on the literary scene and writes monthly for Lithium Magazine. Sophia has had her work published on Rookie Magazine and has also been recognized in several local contests.

Jazzminn Morecraft

Jazzminn Morecraft is currently attending CSU Channel Islands, pursing a degree in English with emphasis in creative writing and a minor in business management. When finished at CI she hopes to pursue a masters in publishing. She works two jobs as the Editor-in-chief of her school paper and holds an internship at SAGE Publications. The ones that means the most to her is her family.

Katrina Mundy

Katrina Mundy is a former police officer turned high school teacher. She has explored herself through writing since she was little, and currently teaches English in Anaheim. By teaching poetry, she hopes to give her students a positive outlet, confidence and an understanding of themselves. She resides in California with her husband, and son.

Emma Owens

Emma Owens was born in a small town in Southern California called Lompoc. She spent her younger days alternating between climbing oak trees and reading books. She has been writing poetry and stories since she was eight years old and intends to continue to do so into her dotage. Presently, she lives in Redmond, Washington with her parents, two siblings, a cat, three dogs, two ferrets, a parrot, and a goat named Bumbler. Her home is not a farm, but it feels like one.

Heather Pease

Heather Pease is a Poet focusing on work centering on feminism, sexuality, identity, culture, mental health, politics and domestic violence. She writes from her own experiences, aiming to give voice to vulnerability, making people think about subjects often stigmatized through society. She writes to empower others whose voices remain unheard. She lives in Orange County, CA with her husband, and two daughters and is currently working on her first book of poems.

Abigail Ramsey

Abigail Ramsey is a writer, editor, and advocate based in Southern California. Her fiction and creative non-fiction attempts to unveil the covert misogyny and white supremacy steeped in Evangelical and Christian cultures. Abigail received her BA in creative writing and certificate in technical writing from California State University, Channel Islands. She currently writes full-time for Pepperdine University celebrating the diverse perspectives and research accomplishments of the university's faculty, staff, and students.

Kennedy Reynolds

Kennedy is a creative, talented 15 year old young woman. While she has always been wiser than her years she is a typical teen that likes face timing and hanging out with friends, going to the beach, traveling and thrifting. She calls her mom her hero and actually believes it.

Helen Rosenau (Your Jewish Fairy Godmother)

Helen Rosenau enjoys a life of goodness, joy, and creativity. She's smart and wise, but still wrestles with patience and discipline. She is the author of *The Messy Joys of Being Human*.

Katin Sarner

Katin Sarner is a highschool senior from Los Angeles with a passion for sharing her story through words. Katin is the co-founder of her non-profit initiative, The Fight Behind Our Forks, educating middle schoolers on eating disorders, body image, and the harms of diet culture. Katin is also a classical singer, most recently having performed at Carnegie Hall. She plans to study Creative Writing and Music in college, and is currently a Junior Editor with Novelly. Katin hopes to finish writing her memoir sometime soon, but in the meantime, her writing has appeared in Harpur Palate, The Hellebore, The Novillian, and HerStry.

Alisha Saxena

Alisha Saxena is an incoming freshman to the University of California, San Diego with a major in Political Science-Public Law. She aspires to play a part in shaping the future of political, cultural, and social development, whether in the United States or internationally. Her favorite mantra is "say positive, stay positive" and it was created through words of inspiration from the most powerful woman in her life-her mother. She hopes the audience enjoys her heartfelt work.

Molly Scott

Molly Scott is a cis queer femme 28-year-old writer and artist from Sonoma County, CA. Molly started writing poetry in middle school after being inspired by Nickelodeon's "As Told By Ginger," and has continued to write poetry as a way to get to know herself, heal from trauma, and cope with mental illness. Molly uses her writing to both find beauty and illustrate the darkness in life, as well as to connect with others who my have similar experiences or who may be able to learn from her writing.

Charlotte Shao

My name is Charlotte Shao, and I am a 15-year-old located in Alhambra, California. I am a mentee in the program WriteGirl and have been published previously in their recent anthology.

Aruni Wijesinghe

Aruni Wijesinghe is a social innovation project manager, substitute ESL teacher, occasional sous chef and erstwhile belly dance instructor. She is an emerging voice in the LA and Orange County poetry scenes and has performed her work at various reading series around Southern California. She has been published by Angels Flight – Literary West, Moon Tide Press, Picture Show Press, Altadena Poetry Review and others. She lives a quiet life with her husband Jeff and their cats Jack and Josie.

COMMUNITY READERS

Thank you to our amazing team of community readers, who volunteered their time to review submissions for *A Teenager's Guide to Feminism.*

Ra Avis

Adam Gilson

Jennifer Ladwig

Kristen Ludwigsen

Denise Morales Soto

Heather Pease

Natasha Popowich

Abigail Ramsey

Henrik Jaron Schneider

Ryan Stevens

Sirisha Vegulla

Xian Wang

Aruni Wijesinghe

Erica Wright

CPSIA information can be obtained
at www.ICGtesting.com
Printed in the USA
FSHW010404281120
76317FS

9 781736 052204